FUQUA

HOW I MADE MY FORTUNE
USING OTHER PEOPLE'S MONEY

J.B. FUQUA

LONGSTREET PRESS

Atlanta

Published by
LONGSTREET PRESS, INC.
2974 Hardman Court
Atlanta, GA 30305

Printed in the United States of America

1st printing 2001

Library of Congress Catalog Card Number: 2001091156

ISBN: 1-56352-680-8

Front cover photograph by: © 1990 Arthur Usherson

Jacket and book design by Burtch Hunter Design

FUQUA

To Dottie, my Madame Queen

CONTENTS

There are many ways to measure a person's life. In the case of J. B. Fuqua, his life's value too often is measured — even by him in this book — by the number of companies he owned, the millions of dollars he earned, and the complex business deals he successfully completed. As amazing as those accomplishments are, they do not adequately reflect the genuine magnitude of his lifetime achievements. J. B. built a remarkably full life of public service, private philanthropy, and genuine caring for family, friends, community, education, capitalism, and much more. Untold thousands have been fortunate enough to be touched by his generosity and kindness. This is the way he should be remembered.

It's too bad he never discovered hobbies outside of work.

J. B.'s book captures much of his life's journey, from a lonely and poor childhood to the pinnacles of power. His myriad accomplishments are all the more amazing because he has battled severe depression for over fifty years. As someone who has also fought this debilitating disease for over twenty years, I know firsthand the quiet pain and life-draining reality of depressive illness. There is no doubt that this struggle too often sapped one of what J. B. calls his three "Big Cs": his capacity to do all he expected of himself in building an even-richer life of accomplishment.

At his side for fifty-six years has been his wonderful Dottie, who deserves a special place in heaven for nurturing J. B. over a lifetime. Married to a workaholic, Dottie brought grace, humor, warmth, comfort, inspiration, and strong-willed determination to their years together. She banished loneliness in his life by bringing so many happy times. (However, J. B. never learned to love parties!)

No story about J. B. would be complete without recognition of what this tall, beautiful, talented, and courageous woman meant to him — and to his success. Even more important has been her dedication to J. B. when he hit the depths of his depression and his other illnesses. She has always been there with him — in moments of triumph and despair — as the steady, firm hand on their family tiller.

While J. B.'s book looks back on their life, it also touches on the splendid legacies of their union, their son Rex and their grandchildren. Rex has achieved a balance in his life that has eluded J. B. While building an independent legacy and his own personal wealth, Rex has also found much more time than his father for family, fun, and a life beyond the numbers. His commitment to philanthropy, to his community, and to education are, however, built upon the tradition that J. B. established throughout his life.

Unquestionably, the most heartbreaking event in the life of Dottie and J. B. was the tragic loss of their other son, Alan, in a plane crash. It nearly tore the life out of them, as it would any parents. J. B. poured himself even more fiercely into his work, while Dottie's private grief was offset by her devotion to raising Rex as their lone surviving child.

J. B. enabled many aspiring politicians to rise to great heights. Carl Sanders became governor of Georgia with his support. J. B.'s generosity has helped the presidential libraries of Jimmy Carter, Gerald Ford, and Lyndon B. Johnson.

The excellent Fuqua School of Business at Duke University serves as the most visible national monument to one man's decision to repay a debt, a debt that J. B. felt he owed Duke for helping him educate himself through its early library loan program.

J. B. has been my close personal friend for more than forty years. My life has been enriched beyond measure by his friendship. In retirement, former President Johnson said he had no closer friend. "J. B. never abandoned me," LBJ once told me. J. B. visited the LBJ Ranch often during the four years Johnson spent in retirement. He always cheered LBJ with stories of business, politics, and Georgia friends.

LBJ said once after J. B.'s plane departed the ranch, "You know, Tom, I've had a few great Georgia friends — Senator

Richard B. Russell, Senator Walter F. George, Governor Carl Sanders, Congressman Carl Vinson, former Secretary of State Dean Rusk, and J. B. There is something about Georgians. They care about you when you are sick, and they come to your funeral when you die."

J. B.'s sleek turbojet was on final approach to the LBJ Ranch on January 23, 1973, loaded with gifts for Lady Bird and LBJ, just as the Johnson family Beechcraft lifted off for a hospital in San Antonio with the lifeless body of the former president inside. Secret Service agents continued to try to revive him. LBJ died suddenly of a heart attack only shortly before J. B. was to visit one last time.

But J. B. did pay his final respects at the LBJ family burial plot at the ranch three days later.

That is J. B. Fuqua — a friend for life. In the best and worst of times, he never forgets those he meets along the way.

His book captures so much of all of this. A quiet, selfless, modest man — yet a giant and a true American hero to those who have been privileged to walk part of his journey with him.

❦

Tom Johnson is the former chairman and CEO of CNN, former publisher of the *Los Angeles Times*, and former executive assistant to President Lyndon B. Johnson. A native of Macon, Georgia, he met J. B. Fuqua in the 1960s and has remained a close friend ever since.

FUQUA

PART
I

THE EARLY YEARS

CHAPTER 1

HARD BEGINNINGS
ON A VIRGINIA FARM

There are some people today who blame their failure to succeed on their deprived childhoods and economic circumstances. I don't subscribe to that belief. I am proof that any obstacle can be overcome if you are willing to educate yourself and work hard.

The words "poor" and "disavantaged" are relative terms, but they accurately describe my childhood. I was raised on a tobacco farm in Prince Edward County, Virginia, in very unhappy circumstances. Two months after I was born on June 26, 1918, in Darlington Heights, my mother died from complications of childbirth and I was taken to her parents to be reared. My mother had anticipated her death and made the arrangements because my father was a tobacco farmer who had no way to raise a baby. My grandparents reared me as their child for all practical purposes, and I did not know the difference until I was older. I called them

Papa and Mama, although they never formally adopted me because I suppose they never considered it necessary.

My birth father was John Brooks Elam and my birth name was John Brooks Elam Jr., but when I grew up I legally changed my name to John Brooks Fuqua, which was my mother's family name, and dropped the junior. But J. B. is what I have always been called. Fuqua is a French name, originally spelled Fouquet. There is a famous restaurant on the Champs-Elysées in Paris with that name. Along the way I suppose somebody got tired of explaining why it was pronounced Fuqua and spelled Fouquet so they changed it.

My father was married three times and outlived all three wives. My mother was his second wife. He had a son from his first marriage — my half-brother — and his situation was the same as mine: My father couldn't take care of the boy and so left him with his wife's parents to rear. He married again after my mother died and had another son, my half-brother Ned Elam, who is now a retired engineer. My father died just short of his 100th birthday. I come from a very long-lived family on both sides so, theoretically, I'm a good risk for an insurance company if I were buying insurance.

My grandparents lived on a farm that was located near Prospect and 10 miles from the county seat of Farmville, a town then and now of about 5,000. My grandparents had several children; all but three were married and all except one was grown when I came along. One of them, my mother's sister, was a mother to me until she was married. It was not an ideal situation for a child, though it was nobody's fault.

There were black tenant families living on the farm who did much of the labor, but I was expected to do chores as soon as I was old enough. Life was especially hard on the farm because we had no tractors or machinery of any kind. We used mules to pull the plows and wagons. The farmhands worked from daylight in the morning to sundown in the afternoon five days a week and a half-day on Saturday. At one point in the Depression when farm prices were at their lowest, I recall we paid our farmhands 50 cents a day. The quality of life of these workers was not much different from what it had been during slavery times.

My earliest memory is of walking two miles to a crossroads called Elam to catch the school bus to go to first grade. To this day, if those paths still existed, I could walk them from my house to Elam blindfolded. I did it so many times that in my mind I have a total map of every little puddle, every tree, everything in the forest from my house to where I caught the bus.

I went to the first consolidated school, where a number of one-room schools had been combined into one school with 11 grades. The school dropout rate was tremendous back then. Of the 25 students who began first grade with me, only nine of us graduated from high school. My school was something of an experiment because it employed teachers in training from what is now Longwood College, who were brought in for three-month sessions and then replaced by other student teachers. That's the way my schooling went until I entered the seventh grade. There, I finally had a full-time teacher named Mrs. Alice Straw, who had taught my mother and who encouraged me greatly. Mrs. Straw had lived with my grandparents before I was born and taught in a red school-house by our home until it was combined with the school I later attended when consolidation took place.

Each of my teachers growing up had a tremendous influence on my life. Sometimes book salesmen came by the school to introduce a new textbook and one of our teachers, Leon Mason, would stand by the window and slowly turn the pages. I asked him one day what he was doing and he said he was reading. I was intrigued, and asked him if he would teach me to read rapidly, which he did. Learning speed reading at age sixteen helped me so much in my constant search for knowledge.

Maude Glenn Raiford was responsible for helping me overcome my shyness by getting me interested in debating and dramatics. To this day, I can get up and speak before 10 people or 10,000 without increasing my heart rate. This ability served me especially well during my 10 years in the political arena.

And, perhaps most importantly, my teacher Boyd Bagby told me how to borrow books through the mail from the Duke University Library. I began to order books on finance and banking and things I did not understand much about. Sometimes I would read a whole book and maybe understand one chapter, but I certainly learned a lot about business before graduating from high school. I think that if I had not had access to those books from Duke and other reading materials, I would certainly have been less successful early on in my business career.

Why did I get interested in business? Well, I knew I did not want to be a farmer because I was born physically lazy. And I noticed when we went to the county seat on Saturdays to get our staples that the bankers and merchants had the biggest automobiles and the biggest homes. That impressed me and influenced my decision to go into business.

I always did very well in school, but I was careful not to get a reputation of being a bookworm or worse, a "smarty-ass." I could have been the valedictorian, but I didn't dare. I made a point not to be number one in my class. While my classmates did their homework every night, I only took my books home on weekends and did all the work then for the following week. I was an avid reader even before I learned about the Duke program and quickly went through every book in our little school library.

I read to get information, but books also were a substitute for my lack of playmates. I was very lonely as a child and I had little in common with the other children at school. There were no boys or girls my age on the farm, either. My grandparents had a son, Wilfred, who was six years older than I, but we were too far apart in age to play together.

Mama was very partial to Wilfred and she made it clear that I was a burden and that she didn't ask for all this to happen. Papa, however, preferred me, and that only added to the tension between my grandparents. It is understandable to me now because they were much too old to raise a child and doing so put a strain on their relationship, but as a child I felt very unwanted. Neither Papa nor Mama ever told me they loved me and I never received the affection that my own children have received or my grandchildren get now. In the summertime, my cousin, Booker Cunningham, occasionally spent time at my house and we became very close. We both recall that we had a favorite cherry tree that we climbed like monkeys when the cherries were ripe. But I do not recall ever having spent the night with a schoolmate or having invited anyone to spend the night with me.

The one toy I remember getting from my father, whom I saw from time to time, was a toy monkey on a string. I never had a bicycle and never learned to ride one. Papa and Mama thought the toys would spoil me, I suppose, and I must say that Wilfred didn't have any toys either, so it wasn't a matter of their depriving only me. For Christmas, we hung a stocking on the mantle in the living room and I would get an orange, some nuts, and some candy in the stocking. And that was Santa Claus. I did get a red American Flyer wagon on one occasion, but it really was more of a tool than a toy because I was expected to use it to haul feed for the animals.

As I mentioned, I was very lonely. My dogs were my only playmates as I roamed the woods and did all the things that young boys do. One of the saddest moments in my childhood was when the first dog I owned died. I put his body in my little wagon, pulled it over the hill and buried him some distance from the house. Sometime later, the mailman, Mr. Gardner, came by and gave me a puppy. I didn't give him a name — he was just a hound — but he became my best friend and accompanied me on many trips to hunt rabbits. Hunting rabbits and squirrels was a big part of life on the farm, of course, and we ate any game we killed.

There were few comforts on the farm. Our house was a plain, two-story structure with weather-boarding. Mama and Papa slept in the first-floor bedroom, which was used as a sitting room during the day, and Wilfred and I shared a bedroom on the second floor. We had a fireplace in the living room/ bedroom combination and wood stoves in the parlor and the kitchen, but there was no heat on the second floor. On cold winter mornings, one did not dawdle getting dressed.

At that time, the Rural Electrical Agency had not yet installed lines so country people could have electricity, and I still remember the terrible odor from a kerosene-operated refrigerator Papa had bought. We had a Delco battery plant, but it was very insufficient compared to the regular electric lines. The batteries furnished 32 volts and had to be charged about twice a week. Almost nothing was made that worked on 32 volts of direct current — no refrigerator, no stove, no radio, just a few dim lightbulbs. In the winter I used the light from the fireplace to read; in the summertime I sat outside on the porch and read until dusk.

One of my favorite places to sit and daydream was in a swing that was attached to the limb of a mimosa tree in the yard. I would swing back and forth thinking about what I might do when my time came to leave the farm. Another favorite place of mine was on one of the poles that was part of the structure we used to hang the hogs when we butchered them.

There were no picnics or family outings except for our trips into Prospect two or three times a week to buy supplies and take care of business. Papa was a county supervisor, which was the same as a county commissioner today, and he took the job very seriously. Watching him campaign kindled my interest in politics and no doubt led to my own political career years later. Papa usually had opposition from his brother-in-law, but he was reelected several times.

I enjoyed going to Farmville, the county seat, with Papa when it was just the two of us because we had an opportunity to have serious talks away from Mama and Wilfred. Once we got to town, we'd get 25-cent haircuts, stop at some of the stores, and visit the county clerk, Horace Adams. We went to town whenever court was in session, and I became fascinated with the trials and arguments in the courtroom. I might have become a lawyer if my life hadn't taken the course it did.

Papa was a very intelligent man and he kept up with the news by reading the daily *Richmond News Leader*, the weekly *Farmville Herald*, *Progressive Farmer*, and *Successful Farmer*, but he never bought a single book as far as I can remember other than the family Bible. He did have a copy of the Code of Virginia law. When people came by the house with a question about the law, he would take out the Code and look it up. It was ironic that I would become such a bookworm when I was reared in a home without a single book except the Bible.

Otherwise, life on the farm was mostly hard work and

little fun. As soon as I was old enough, I was taught to hitch up the mules and plow the fields. Like other kids my age back then, I rarely wore shoes and I know exactly what Jimmy Carter meant when he wrote in his memoir that you haven't lived until you've felt the freshly turned soil on your bare feet.

Most of my chores involved getting the tobacco crop planted and harvested. I was responsible for helping sow the seeds in the woods where we had dug up and enclosed an area with a 25-foot-square frame. Once the plants grew to a certain size, they were transplanted to the field like tomato plants. Tobacco was the cash crop, but we also had corn and wheat. It was hard work plowing the rows to get rid of the weeds and keep soil around the roots. Tobacco worms were a constant problem and had to be killed before they chewed big holes in the leaves and decreased the value. We used a mixture of insecticide and lime in bags that we shook over the tops of the plants, but I still had to pick and kill large numbers of these ugly worms by hand. Another nasty job was suckering tobacco, where you pinched off the little leaves and stems until your hands were covered with sticky juice.

Harvesting and preparing the crop for market was another difficult task. This was usually done in late August when we picked the leaves and hung them on sticks in tobacco barns to be cured. This was done over a slow fire that we kept going with old railroad ties. We would continue the process for several weeks until the leaves turned a rich chocolate color. The tobacco we raised was used for snuff, chewing tobacco, and cigars, but not for cigarettes.

All the tobacco we grew was auctioned, whether it was 10 pounds or 1,000 pounds. We would take it to the warehouse and put it in big baskets that were lined up for the tobacco buyers and auctioneers to inspect. Each basket had already been weighed. After the auctioneer was finished, the buyers would add up the figures and pay the farmers on the spot.

I hated farming and I would have considered doing anything to get off the farm. Even if I had wanted to stay, I realized at an early age that the farm wouldn't be big enough to support another family. And, since Wilfred was older than me and the natural heir, he would get preference.

Fortunately, something happened when I was about 14 or 15 that changed the course of my life. We had just gotten our first radio and the rest of the family had gone to Farmville for the day and left me at home alone. I started playing around with the dial until I came across a station in Richmond where the chief engineer was teaching a course in Morse code. At the end of the program, he announced that anyone who was interested could mail him 25 cents and he would send them a book entitled *How to Become an Amateur Radio Operator*. Well, I sent my money and soon received a booklet explaining how to buy radio parts from a mail order house and make my own radio receiver. That 25 cents was the greatest investment of my life. I learned Morse code and before long I was able to order enough parts to build a transmitter.

When I began assembling my radio, I didn't have a soldering iron to connect the wires. They probably only cost a dollar or so at the time, but I didn't have that much money.

Instead, I made my own using an iron rod with a corncob handle. To heat it, I opened the door to the firebox in the kitchen stove and held the iron rod in the fire until it turned red. I almost burned a hole in my hand many times holding it that way. Once the rod was hot enough, I used it to melt the solder and make the connections. It was pretty crude, but it worked. I didn't realize at the time what a good example it was of making use of what you have to accomplish your goals.

Because nobody in the family was interested in my radio, I had to get some of the farmhands to help me string up the antenna wire the required distance between two poles. Next, I read every book on radios I could find. When I got my ham radio license I began "talking" with people all over the world using Morse code and my tiny one-tube transmitter that operated off of batteries. Some ham operators were just beginning to use voice transmissions, but I didn't have a microphone or the money or the 110-volt electricity to even dream of doing that. Using my call letters — W3E00 — I would transmit messages hoping that someone would hear them and respond. Once you made contact, you would have a conversation about your location or the kind of equipment you had and agree to exchange USL cards that listed your call letters.

My little ham radio opened up horizons to me that I had only imagined, but none of my high school classmates shared my enthusiasm. They didn't understand and they didn't care about my hobby. This really didn't bother me, though, for once I sat down at that little radio in our pump room, I was in hog heaven. I also realized that my ham radio was my ticket out of Prospect.

One of the reasons for my success is that I have prepared myself every step of the way. Before I became a manager, I had read many books on management. I have always been prepared for the next phase of my life. In other words, I made sure I had the knowledge to succeed. As I headed toward high school graduation, I decided my next step was to find a job as a radio operator. I knew I had the capacity to get that job. As far as capital, I relied on income from the few rows of tobacco Papa had let me tend to and treat as my own. And, as a lonely young man eager to find my place in the world, my courage was boundless.

CHAPTER 2

STRIKING OUT ON MY OWN

Because a college education was out of the question for me, I went to Norfolk, Virginia, after graduation to take an examination for a commercial radio operator's license. The exam was difficult, but I had studied diligently and passed with no trouble. Afterward, the Federal Communications Commission (FCC) official who gave me the exam explained that the best way to get a job was by applying at RCA. He said that company employed most of the radio operators on ships.

I turned in my application and a few weeks later a messenger came around from Prospect with a telegram advising me to call a number in Norfolk about a job on a ship. This may be hard to believe today, but I had never spoken on a telephone. Taylor's Store in Prospect had the only telephone in the area, so I went there, showed the telegram to the lady clerk,

"Miss Etta," and asked her to make the call. After she made the connection, the man in Norfolk said he had a job as a radio operator on a freighter if I could be there on the following Sunday afternoon. He told me the ship was sailing to South Africa, but I was so excited it wouldn't have made any difference to me where it was going. All I cared about was that I was finally going to get off the farm.

I was still excited when I got to Norfolk the next Sunday and boarded the SS *Sagadahoc*. The man who greeted me took me aboard, showed me the radio equipment, and said, "You know how to operate this stuff, so good luck." Here I was, a 17-year-old kid away from home for the first time, and I was the only radio operator on the ship. The ship took off that night to go down the coast to Tampa and Mobile and New Orleans and on to South Africa with a load of cars, lumber, and general cargo. I was nervous, but the farther I got away from the farm, the happier I became.

That first voyage was an important phase of my education. One of the things I learned was the value of persistence. I still have an old Underwood typewriter in my office at home to remind me of that lesson. The first night out at sea, I knew I had to copy the weather information and give it to the captain of the ship. After I wrote it down in longhand and took it to him on the bridge, he looked at it for a moment, handed it back to me, and said, "Young man, don't ever bring me anything again that's not typed." The problem, of course, was that I couldn't type. I did know that there was a typewriter in the radio room and I had a chart that showed where to put your fingers on the keys. I practiced ALL night and by morning had learned to type without looking at the keys.

I knew my business concerning the radio, but initially I had problems with the ship's crew treating me as an outcast. I didn't figure out why until a little later. I wasn't aware of it when I came on board, but there was a strike of radio operators going on and I was considered a strikebreaker for taking the job. Once I recognized the problem, I went down to the union headquarters when we got to Tampa and paid five dollars for a membership. Technically, I was still a strikebreaker, but the crew accepted me because I was now a union member.

Life on the boat with a crew of rough, older men was pretty tough for a young man like myself. We would be at sea for 30 days and when we got to port the men would draw their pay and make up for being out to sea all that time. They would hit the bars and go drinking and engage in other things that sailors did to relieve the tension. I never did any of that. I didn't drink and I didn't want to waste my money. Occasionally I would do some sightseeing, but mostly I stayed on the ship and read. That was another benefit of my job. The radio operator was in charge of the ship's library and got to select a new collection of books on every trip. Reading was much more enjoyable — and cheaper — than hitting all the bars with the crew. I read biographies and books on radio, banking, economics, and other subjects that were not usually of interest to kids my age. Getting information was what interested me. I would never read a novel if I could find something else.

My job as a ship radio operator was a good one by any measure. I was paid $90 a month and got a uniform, good food, and a comfortable bunk bed. On the other hand, I was on duty 24 hours a day doing nothing most of the time except listening for other ships or shore stations to call my ship. Our identification call letters on the SS *Sagadahoc* were KTUO and the code, or dots and dashes, for this was K (- . -) T (-) U (. . -) O (- - -). To this day, I can "read" Morse code almost as fast or as well as when I was a professional radio operator. Other youth out of high school with no skills made $12 to $18 per week and had to pay for room and board, clothes, and other things. Since I had almost no living expenses, I saved most of what I made so I could get on with my ambitions for a career. This was not simply a matter of luck. I had prepared myself for this job by studying books and learning to be a commercial radio operator.

On the ship, everyone called me "Sparks." In those days, all radio operators were known as "Sparks" because the first transmitters were operated with coils instead of vacuum tubes, and a spark would leap between the two coils. Like other radio operators on other ships, I was classified as an officer and ate in the officers' mess, where the food was excellent. Of course, this meant being properly dressed and using good manners. The captain was a Norwegian who was extremely strict about neatness and cleanliness. The habits I formed on the ship served me well later in my business career.

My duties as a radio operator were not that demanding. Mostly they involved listening to weather reports and communications about the cargo and where it was to go. Another of my duties, for which I received extra pay, was keeping the payroll for the dozen officers and 30 crewmen. Since I had no place to spend any money on the ship and never went drinking with the men when we hit port, I saved basically all my pay.

One of the benefits of being in the Merchant Marine was the opportunity to visit many exotic places. I did a lot of sightseeing in cities in Africa such as Capetown and Durban and even got to go into the bush and view the wild animals. It was a good life for some people, but after a year I decided to leave the Merchant Marine to seek my fortune on dry land.

CHAPTER 3

STARTING MY CAREER IN RADIO
AND TELEVISION

When I got out of the Merchant Marine, I knew I wanted to work at a radio station. I was qualified legally to do the work with my commercial radio operator's license, but finding a job without technical school training was going to be difficult. With that in mind, I prepared myself by enrolling in the Capitol Radio Engineering Institute in Washington, D.C., and taking classes for several months. Since I had saved most of my salary from the freight boats, I was able to pay my way through technical school with no problem.

Once I completed my course, I applied to a whole slew of radio stations. Out of the dozens of letters I wrote to the chief engineers of these stations, I received only one postcard back from WIS in Columbia, South Carolina, offering me a job as a summer relief operator. In other words, they needed someone to fill in for the engineers when they took their two weeks' vacation. I knew it was temporary and that I would be out of work in a month or two, but my savings were about to run out. So I took the job.

As it happened, things worked out better than expected. I went to work in July 1937 as a temporary engineer and by the end of 1938 I had impressed the management so much they hired me as chief engineer of another station under the same ownership, WCSC in Charleston. Understand that this was not merely a case of being in the right place at the right time. I was ambitious and prepared for each one of these jobs.

Before long, I began to think I was just as smart as the manager of the station and I thought if he could manage a radio station, I could manage one, too. He was much older than I was, but I had great confidence in my abilities even at 21. I've always had a big ego and I've never trusted anyone who didn't have one also. If you don't think well of yourself, how can you expect others to?

My next step was to make a business plan. I looked at three cities: Augusta, Georgia; Columbus, Georgia; and Roanoke, Virginia. After determining that Augusta was the most favorable location for a second radio station, I headed there with nothing but a used car and some pieces of paper on which I had projected how much it would cost to build and operate a new station. Knowing no one in Augusta, I went to the Chamber of Commerce and asked the secretary, Lester Moody, to help me locate some investors. Anybody else would have thrown me out of his office, but Mr. Moody was patient and kind and helpful. He picked up the phone and made some calls, and before the end of the day he had found three men who were willing to endorse my note for $10,000 to build the radio station. The three investors who put up the money to build WGAC were Glenn Boswell, the general manager of the *Augusta Herald*; Milwee Owens, editor of the *Augusta Herald*; and F. Fred Kennedy, a lawyer. Kennedy later became my partner in the Royal Crown Bottling Co. and subsequently was a superior court judge until his death. As part of the agreement, I would own 10 percent of the radio station and would be the general manager with a salary of $250 a month. And that's how I got into the radio business without using any of my own money. I didn't invest any money because I didn't have any. All I had was a vision and an abundance of self-confidence.

When I started WGAC in 1940, it was the second radio station in Augusta, but it was profitable from day one. Most stations back then played a variety of music in an attempt to offer something for everyone's taste. They played hillbilly music one hour and the next hour they might play classical music. By today's standards, it was kind of stupid not to realize that you should find a niche and cater to it.

I had the NBC network, which carried the national news. There wasn't much local news coverage — we didn't have teams of reporters running around like radio stations do today. Usually someone (often me) would write up a news report they had copied out of the local newspaper and read it on the air.

By 1946, WGAC was doing so well that I built another radio station — WFAK — in Charleston. I hired a young man named Tom Hennessy who was working at that station to come to Augusta and be an announcer. He proved to be an invaluable addition to my team, and moved with me as I acquired other businesses over the years.

In 1949, I sold my interest in WGAC and bought 100 percent of another station in Augusta, WTNT — "Dynamite in Dixie." I got the money to buy WTNT through one of the best deals I ever made and once again I did it by using other people's money. One night I had invited Fred Kennedy over for dinner. During the course of the evening, Kennedy told me that the Royal Crown Bottling Company could be bought because the elderly man who owned it had what was then called an "unwarranted surplus" tax problem: he had not paid out the earnings as dividends because the tax rate on dividends was almost confiscatory during World War II, and he had accumulated a large amount of cash. In reality, the only way the owner of a business could take the earnings from a corporation was to sell the business.

This was too good an opportunity to pass up. At 8 o'clock the next morning, I was sitting in the Royal Crown owner's office. We initially agreed on a deal by which I would pay him $125,000 for the business, but he seemed reluctant to sell and changed his mind. I finally realized the problem. What he wanted more than the money was a place to go every day to meet his buddies, and he did not want to sell the business at any price unless he could retain his office. Once I understood this, I offered to draw up a contract that provided that he could keep the same office he presently occupied for as long as we owned the business. We settled on that point and that's how I bought the Royal Crown Bottling Co.

It worked out that the purchase price of the company was about the same amount as the cash that had been accumulated. By selling all of his stock in the corporation to us, the owner received capital gains treatment of the transaction, and the capital gains rate was very low. I, in turn, used his accumulated cash to buy his business — I put up NO CASH.

I was under no obligation to bring Fred Kennedy into the deal, but since I was not putting up any cash, I thought it would only be fair if I offered him the opportunity to be a part of it if he wanted. He, too, saw the possibilities when I explained to him how it would work, and so we drew up a partnership agreement whereby we had an equal interest. We also had a provision that required either party to offer his 50 percent to the other partner if he decided to sell. This clause is commonly called the right of first refusal.

The Royal Crown Bottling Company made a good profit. We took cash out of it every month, even though we had not put a penny of capital in it. After some years, however, the bottling equipment became obsolete and needed to be replaced. The new equipment would be quite expensive, but it could be easily financed internally. When I brought the matter up to

Kennedy, he opposed the plan because he was not willing to stop the cash flow he had been getting each month. We badly needed to modernize, but in order to go ahead with the deal, I saw that I would have to buy Kennedy out. I also knew that Kennedy's pride was so great that he could not bear to walk down Broad Street in Augusta with people knowing that I had bought him out.

When I talked to the loan officer at Citizens & Southern Bank about borrowing $100,000 to buy out Kennedy, he agreed that Kennedy would never allow this deal to happen. The banker agreed to loan me the money on the condition that he also arrange a similar loan for Kennedy in case he wanted to buy me out. With that under-standing, I went to Kennedy and offered him $100,000 for his half-interest in Royal Crown. As expected, he turned it down and insisted that he would buy me out. Since I had already laid the groundwork for him to get the loan from the bank without putting up any money, he was able to buy my half.

As it turned out, it was a good deal for both of us. He continued to operate the company profitably for a number of years. And with the $100,000 that I got for my half-interest in Royal Crown, I was financially able to buy my own radio station and get out of the 10 percent partnership agreement at WGAC.

By that time, there were four radio stations in Augusta and the one that was the least profitable was WTNT, which was owned by Walter Brown of Spartanburg, South Carolina, and one of the Knox brothers from Thomson. Because of the station's dismal financial picture, I had no trouble convincing Walter Brown to sell me WTNT for $75,000.

When I told the staff at WGAC that I was leaving to take over WTNT, there was much sincere regret and some feelings of apprehension about what that would mean for them. They did not know whether WGAC would cut back their salaries or make changes in the work rules that would not be popular. Almost every one of them approached me privately and asked to go with me to WTNT, even though it was the bottom station in the market. Some of them had the idea that I was the genius who had made WGAC successful and they wanted to be with the genius.

Because I did not have a noncompete agreement with WGAC, I was free to take any of the personnel I wanted. Thus I was able to bring the top people from WGAC and in effect start our operation at WTNT with a staff who could bring advertising revenue with them, as well as provide the listeners with quality programming. We changed the call letters to WJBF and in the first month of operation we had more revenue than WTNT had had in any three-month period.

Meanwhile, business deteriorated at WGAC after I left. The owners made a mistake by bringing in a general manager to take my place who was not from Augusta or the South and who had no experience in running a job of that sort.

While I had managed WGAC very well, I found it more of a challenge to own WJBF because I took over a physical facility that was far inferior to the facilities of WGAC.

WGAC was 5000 watts on the low end of the dial and it had several times the coverage of WJBF. We dealt with that problem by selling WJBF's advertisers on the idea that it was more important for them to cover the immediate area in Augusta and vicinity. In other words, we convinced them that all the coverage WGAC had was not necessary for a targeted audience.

Another of my challenges was to move the one-hour slot of Procter & Gamble–sponsored soap operas from WGAC to WJBF. I had worked so hard to get the soap operas at WGAC and now I had to persuade the people at Procter & Gamble to move them to a station that had less coverage and a smaller audience. WJBF did have the advantage of being an NBC affiliate, however, and the soap operas were NBC programs. I had been carrying them on WGAC as recordings, but all I had to do was throw a switch to get them at WJBF since they were on the network.

Soap operas were the number-one daytime audience-getters in Augusta and I wanted them for that reason. Convincing Procter & Gamble to switch to a station with less coverage took some doing, but I finally worked things out to everyone's satisfaction. It was a matter of salesmanship, but I wasn't a typical slap-them-on-the-back type of salesman. I simply made my sales pitch as a typed presentation based on the cost versus the number of people reached. Getting the soap operas was the making of WJBF because I now had the most profitable daytime program.

R E X   F U Q U A

"Looking back at Dad's career, I think what made him a good salesman was that he was always totally prepared. And instead of taking the route many salesmen take when they are fun-loving, likable people, his approach was, 'I'm going to leave having these people know that I know so much about their product or about what they want that they can't say no.' He impressed them with his intellect."

I made other changes that proved to be successful as well. When I took over WTNT, I not only changed the call letters to WJBF, I changed the format from recorded music to a full-network program operation with a variety of shows. When the ratings came in, I was home free because the station's share of the audience was as great or greater than that of any of the other three stations in Augusta.

The soap operas were a major factor in the success of WJBF, but so were the seasoned sales staff and the amount of promotion we did. One of the reasons I have been so successful in my business ventures is that I know how to use advertising and promotion to bring attention to a product or business. For example, in the early 1960s, WJBF bought a small radio station, WEOA, in Evansville, Indiana. The first thing I did was change the call letters from WEOA to

WROZ. I used a clever piece of artwork to go with the letters WROZ and I called the station Rosy Radio. It was not long after I got the station that everyone in the Evansville area knew about Rosy Radio.

Advertising and promotion are things that are overlooked by many in management. When business begins to drop off, people too often takes the view that advertising budgets should be cut. Often that is the last move before bankruptcy. Advertising and marketing are usually the last expenses you should cut in almost any kind of business.

We never stinted on spending for promotional events at WJBF. One of our most successful of these was our sponsorship of the annual arrival of Santa Claus the day after Thanksgiving. Just having Santa show up at a store would not have been exciting enough, so we arranged for him to arrive by parachuting out of a plane. Actually, the Santa the kids saw jumping out of the plane was a professional parachutist dressed in a red suit so he would look like the real thing from the ground. Once he landed, he would switch places with the real Santa who was waiting nearby. It was a big deal for kids and their parents and it never failed to generate interest in our station.

Another popular event was our July Fourth fireworks display. We bought the equipment necessary at a relatively inexpensive price and then we went all out to provide the most colorful and spectacular fireworks. We did many things of that type to call attention to the station and they all worked to our benefit. Not only did we have the largest audience, but we had by far the most advertising volume of any of the radio stations in Augusta.

THE DAWN OF TELEVISION

In the early days of television, few people had the foresight to invest in this new medium, but I had made up my mind to own a television station when I saw my first TV set in 1939 at the New York World's Fair. I determined then that television was going to be the thing of the future for communication, entertainment, and advertising.

In 1950, I had one of the few television receivers in Augusta. I had a three-story home, and on the roof I had constructed an antenna system that looked like it might belong at a military installation. I could only get one station, WBT in Charlotte, and the technology was such that WBT did not always show a picture, but when it did, it attracted kids from all over our neighborhood.

I was ready to get into television that year, but the Korean War was on and there was a freeze on licenses. I didn't want to be held up for a single minute, however, so I dug around and found out there was a whole television station's worth of equipment in a warehouse in Dallas, Texas. I bought that equipment, as well as a tower and antenna from Cincinnati, and sent a truck to bring everything to Augusta so I would be prepared when the Korean War ended.

When the right opportunity came along later in 1950, I applied for a television license and got the Channel 6 slot. Television was so new that not many people were applying for

TV rights in smaller markets, but I still encountered some competition for the WJBF-TV license from the Martin brothers who owned Martin Theaters Co. in Columbus, Georgia.

CARL PATRICK, PRESIDENT OF MARTIN THEATERS AND LATER CEO OF FUQUA INDUSTRIES

"Martin Theaters had a lot of money in the bank, and we wanted to get into the television business. Augusta was a two-station market, and we decided to apply for a license. The other applicant for Channel 6 was J. B. Fuqua, with a net worth of $80,000. We didn't think he would have much of a chance to get the license, so we sent a man up to Augusta to get the elevations for the tower and other information. It eventually came to pass that I ran into J. B. and he said, 'You know, I can beat you in a hearing.' I said, 'J. B., you're going to spend more than your $80,000 just getting to a hearing. Then when you get there, you're not going to have anything.' He said, 'Well, I'm local. That's in my favor.' Neither of us wanted a long, drawn-out fight, so we talked about a bargain. Finally, I said, "J. B., how'd you like to have $100,000 tax free?" Well, he worked his slide rule back and forth and we made a deal right there wherein Martin Theaters got one-third interest in the application."

WJBF-TV went on the air on Thanksgiving Day 1953 with ceremonies and speeches from the usual dignitaries. What I remember about that day was a little embarrassing. When it came my turn to make a speech, a fly lit on my nose. It must have been a good omen, though, because WJBF became one of my most profitable enterprises.

In 1953, not many people had television sets, simply because there were not that many stations. As more stations went on the air, sales of TV sets rocketed and so did our advertising revenue. I had a network contract with NBC, which was number one at that time, and I carried local programming, as well as all of the most popular network shows: *The Milton Berle Show, The Big Picture, Colgate Comedy Hour, Amos and Andy, Life of Riley, Name That Tune,* and the football game of the week.

The technology in those days was very crude compared to what we have now. We didn't have videotape, and the first television cameras were huge things that weighed several hundred pounds. The only thing you could do if you wanted to have a record of something was to film it and then televise the film. We had no tape, so if we wanted to show a delayed program, it was done by something called a kinescope, which was a 16mm picture taken off the screen of a television set. Needless to say, the quality of the picture was quite poor.

In the early days of television, everything was live. Local commercials were based on what we thought they ought to look like, and a lot of mistakes were made.

TOM HENNESSY, ANNOUNCER AND WJBF EXECUTIVE

"Around 1954, one of the fashion shops in town bought a half-hour show, and the owner's wife was going to do the commentary, which is never good. We were trying to be fancy and dress things up, and we wanted something that looked like stone pillars from ancient Rome. All we had was a cardboard model of these things that looked real on camera. In order to create a backdrop, we used something that was nothing more than a big roll of paper that you unwound. It was a convex shape and it would stand on its own without any support as long as nobody touched it.

"So we set the studio up with two cardboard 'stone' columns and the backdrop. Before we went on the air, I talked to the girls who would be modeling the outfits and told them there was nothing holding up the backdrop except the shape. I told them the slightest little pressure would make it fall.

"The shop owner's wife sits down at a microphone in the studio and begins reading the script for each girl's dress. Well, the third girl comes out with a big bouffant dress and forgets her instructions and brushes up against the backdrop. I can start to see it fall and there's nothing I can do about it. Sure enough, it falls over and hits her on the back of the head. Of course, it didn't weigh anything, it's just paper, but it shocked her. And she ran off, leaving the backdrop to knock the pillars down. We faded to black and threw up the store's logo and the guy's wife is still reading the script."

There were other mistakes that were quite laughable, but generally the advertisers didn't mind. Our commercials were well thought of and well thought out, and I had good talent both on and off the air.

Many of the big names in television got started in Augusta and other small markets. On Channel 6 we hired a fellow named Jim Nabors to splice film. He later became a famous singer and actor who played Gomer Pyle on what was then the number-one network show. Another celebrity who appeared regularly on WJBF early in her career was singer Brenda Lee. She was popular then and she still is.

REX FUQUA

"It was great fun having a father who owned a television station. We got to meet a lot of celebrities; they were usually country music singers who came through town. I used to run the camera at the station on Sunday morning. They felt comfortable starting me off with the gospel music programs such as the Lewis Family. I guess they thought if I made a mistake it wouldn't matter."

The news programming, which Jim Davis took charge of in 1960, was pretty pathetic compared to what it is now. Jim had one other person working with him and, since there were no TelePrompTers, he had to read the news off a sheet of paper and look up at the camera every so often. We had some 16mm film that we used to shoot some events, but real news coverage didn't exist until the '70s.

JIM DAVIS, RETIRED NEWS DIRECTOR FOR WJBF-TV

"Two things stand out in my mind about working with J. B. After he moved to Atlanta, he would still come back to Augusta once a month to meet with the department heads at a lunch at the Pinnacle Club. At one of those luncheons, he leaned back in his chair and said, 'What have you done about minority employment? I don't mean menial types, I'm talking about on-air personnel.' John Raddick, who was station manager, was sitting beside me. He said, 'J. B., they're awfully hard to find trained.' He said, 'It's your job to train them. I think we'd better start doing it before the government tells us we have to start doing it.' So we hired Frank Thomas as a news reporter. He was the first black newsman in Augusta, except for the black radio stations. That was one of the things J. B. did that impressed me very much.

"A year or so later at one of these luncheons, J. B. named a date and said, 'After that, we will accept no more cigarette advertisements.' We were the first station in the country to take that position. He said, 'I know it's going to be a loss of revenue, but I think this is going to be the trend. We'll have to make up the revenue somewhere else.' Of course, J. B. personally did not like smoking."

Our television commercials cut into our radio revenues somewhat, but we began selling the commercials with the idea that TV and radio were complementary to each other. The WJBF radio station continued to be profitable, and after a few years I sold it to a man in North Carolina who had never been in the business. WJBF stayed on the air for many years until it eventually lost much of its audience to FM stations and folded.

Augusta had only two television stations then — 6 and 12 — but when other ultrahigh frequency stations came in later, the city got one or two of those. Under federal regulations, you could only own one station in a market. If I could have anticipated what was going to happen, I would have bought a UHF station in some other market, but in those early days it looked like UHF stations were not going to be able to have enough coverage. It was a hard sell attracting advertisers for UHF stations, but when cable television was developed and the cable companies were required to carry all the local broadcasting stations, UHF stations became almost as valuable as VHF ones.

BUTCH CAMPBELL, FORMER PRESIDENT OF WJBF-TV

"Back when I was a director, we had what we called a simulcast with our other television station, which was picking up a show from us at a precise time every day. One day I'm in there and my engineer cannot be found. I had to figure out how to patch the wires in so the other television station could pick us up. I could not for the life of me figure out how to do that. I went in there and said, 'Mr. Fuqua, can you help me?' He walked in there to the patch panel and figured it out in about 30 seconds. He always said he used other people's money and other people's brains, but he used other people's brains after he had used his, I can tell you that. He set the wheels in motion and relied on other people to keep them going. He would allow you to do your job. And if you didn't do it, you would know about it."

YOUNG BUSINESSMAN ON THE RISE

Once the TV station was up and running, I continued to get involved in all sorts of side businesses. Early on, I had established my credibility by borrowing money to buy a real estate lot, building a house, and paying the money back. I would then use the profits to buy another lot, build another house, and repeat the process until the people at the banks knew me and trusted me to repay my debts.

REX FUQUA

"I think that Dad was successful because he didn't know any better sometimes, or didn't worry about going to somebody and asking them something. He didn't know that people were not supposed to do that. He was courageous and self-confident and, because he grew up as a farm boy and wasn't familiar with the rules of business, he felt he could make his own rules. That benefited him early on. If you have one or two successes, that gives you the confidence to try other things. His idea about creating a credit history for himself is quite interesting. You listen to talk-show host Clark Howard on WSB radio here in Atlanta today and he's saying the same thing."

Along the way, I had also gotten into the insurance business because of my friendship with Ed Willingham, who owned his own company, Willingham Insurance Co. Ed, who was in automobile financing and insurance, became my best friend. He was a young man, but he had heart trouble. One day on the street he propped himself up against the wall in front of his office and asked me if I would look after his company and take care of his brother if he died. Ed did not want his widow to lose everything if a bank took over the business. His brother was not as bright as Ed was, and Ed recognized he wouldn't have the ability to make it on his own. Of course I told Ed I would handle things, but I didn't anticipate that he would die so soon. He dropped dead a few months later in Chicago on his way to the Mayo Clinic.

When I took over Willingham Finance Co., I thought I could liquidate it right away, but it wasn't that simple. I would have to start a new company in the same business. So here I am, selling insurance policies and borrowing money from various banks for the auto finance company. I would borrow money at 6 percent and lend it out at 12 percent. I had to go from bank to bank in Augusta, Atlanta, and New York, and I had to kowtow to banks so much that I determined that one day I was going to get into the banking business to see what it was all about. And I eventually did just that when I bought Georgia Federal Savings and Loan in the 1980s.

I never liked the finance business, however, and I sold Willingham Finance Co. after about four years. The idea of people coming in every week and paying on their furniture and cars just didn't suit my nature.

CHAPTER 4

STARTING A FAMILY

The best deal I ever made was marrying Dorothy "Dottie" Chapman. I was working at WGAC in Augusta in 1944 and my closest personal friend was Donald "Squash" Kelly, who was the sales manager of the radio station. Occasionally, he and his wife Elsie — we called her "Doodles" — would invite me to dinner. I was single and I was always looking for an invitation to go out or do anything else fun. The war was going on and there were many more girls around than there were fellows. Single men were always in demand for dinner parties where there would be single women. So scarce were young males because of the draft that at one point I had virtually an all-female staff at the radio station.

I had been drafted like other young men, but I wasn't called up for active duty. Because of my technical experience in radio,

I was offered an opportunity to train Signal Corps enlistees at Fort Gordon. After working at my regular job managing WGAC radio by day, I went to Augusta Vocational School five nights a week to teach soldiers, who ranged from grammar school dropouts to college graduates, how to test and repair Army radio equipment. This was a very challenging job because there was such a wide range of education, aptitude, and interest among these men.

After the war was over, I was heartened to learn that several of my students had gotten jobs in some type of technical work after they were discharged from the military. They thanked me for teaching them a skill that enabled them to get out of the textile mills and into better jobs.

Had I gone into the military, it is unlikely that I would be writing this book or any book. I would have been made a radio operator on one of the ships that made the run through the North Atlantic to Murmansk, Russia. A very high percentage of these ships were sunk by the Germans.

Anyway, because I was one of the few single men in Augusta in 1944, Squash and Doodles asked me to dinner at their home to meet a young woman who worked for Ed Willingham of Willingham Finance Company. That's when I first met Dottie, but I didn't get to talk to her much that night because I spent most of the evening fixing the Kellys' radio, which had been giving them trouble. Incidentally, I found out later that she had been invited as a substitute for another girl.

DOTTIE FUQUA

"I lived with some other girls in Augusta during the war. We called it Duration Domicile. The wife of a friend who worked for J. B. called one of the girls and asked if she could come and have dinner with them and J. B. Fuqua. She said they had some black-market steaks. She said , 'Oh, I wish I could, but my mother and father are coming to town and we're going to dinner and to a movie.' She said, 'Well, ask one of the other girls.' Two of them worked at night, so another girl and I spoke up and said, 'Yes, we'll go.' Well, the other girl was serious about a boy overseas, so I went from work. J. B. spent the whole evening working on the radio. I came home and said, 'I'd have been better off reading a book.' I didn't get to know him at all. It was six weeks before I saw him again. One night he called the office about 6 o'clock and asked me to go to dinner with him. I said, 'I'm sorry but I'm busy. I can't go.' I had asked my boss Ed Willingham and his wife to come have some ham and eggs and grits with my aunt and me that night. When I hung up the phone, Ed says, 'Who was that?' And I said, 'It was J. B. Fuqua.' He said, 'What did he want?' Well, I told him and he said, 'Why don't you go? The finest young man in town and you won't go out with him?' I told Ed that if J. B. really wanted a date, he could call earlier than 6 P.M. But we finally had a date, and it was a whirlwind courtship after that."

I was impressed with Dottie. I grew more impressed the better I got to know her. We became engaged in December 1944 and on February 10, 1945, we were married. But everything did not go as smoothly before the ceremony as we thought it would.

DOTTIE FUQUA

"The Wednesday before we were to be married, J. B.'s friends gave him a bachelor party at a lodge. They had never seen him 'tight' at all, so they decided they were going to get him drunk. When he thought they were sobering him up with coffee, they actually were putting whiskey in the coffee. He called me the next morning and said, 'I don't feel so good. I have a backache.' I said, 'I bet you ache all over.' The landlady called later and said she thought he really was ill. We called the doctor and it turns out J. B. was having a kidney stone attack. I went to see him in the hospital and I said, 'We're going to have to postpone the wedding.' He said, 'No, I'm going to do it if I have to walk down the aisle with a needle in my arm.' Later, at the rehearsal party, I was almost in tears when one of J. B.'s business partners, Glenn Boswell, brought him to the rehearsal dinner. J. B. was determined we weren't going to postpone the wedding."

Because gas for cars was rationed during the war, we decided we would fly my plane to Miami for our honeymoon. The trip turned out to be more eventful than we expected. We could not fly at night, so I had gotten an employee at the radio station to fly the plane to Columbia earlier. After the wedding, we drove to Columbia to pick up the plane and arranged for the employee to drive my car back to Augusta. The following day we left for Florida, but the headwind was so strong we could barely make any progress. We had only gotten about 50 miles when we decided to stop and spend the night in Aiken, South Carolina.

The next day we made it as far as Jacksonville, Florida, but we had another interesting experience there. As we approached the city airport, I kept calling the control tower on my radio without getting any response. Since we were low on fuel, I decided to go ahead and land anyway. As we came down on the runway, a soldier in a Jeep taxied alongside the plane. When we stopped, he told me that the airport had been converted to a military field and private aircraft were not allowed. However, upon learning that we were both from the Augusta area, he became more accommodating and directed me to another airfield nearby that had facilities for private aircraft. After we landed and refueled at this airfield, which had unpaved runways, by the way, we decided to leave the plane and take the train to Miami the next day.

Travel was considerably less expensive in those days. When we stayed in the Columbia Hotel, which was the best in town, it cost $7 a night. At the Normandy Plaza in Miami

Beach, also one of the best hotels, we paid $120 for six nights. In 1940, I was making $250 a month, plus a share of the profits from the radio station. That was good money for that time.

The trip back was less eventful. I had taught Dottie to navigate the plane by using what is called a sectional map. This is a map that has roads and railroads and all types of landmarks on the ground. The idea was to plot your course and fly from one checkpoint to another. Dottie became quite good at it and, in many ways, she has been the navigator in our marriage for more than 56 years.

Dottie never worked outside the home, but she helped me in every way she could. Our first child was Rex and he was born in 1949, four years after we were married. Our second son Alan came along two years later. They brought us such joy. The greatest void in our lives was not having more children.

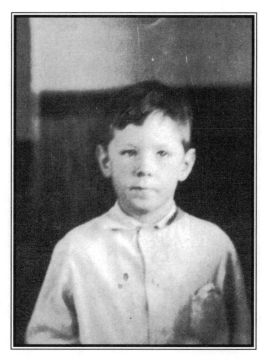

Here I was as a small child in the 1920s.

The house in Virginia where I lived with my grandparents.

I was a real farm boy during my younger years.

The proverbial "goose that laid the golden egg":
the original ham radio I built at age 15 that changed my life.

Here I was aboard the S.S. *Sagadahoc* at age 17
on Christmas Day, 1935.

I was the Chief Engineer at WCSC in Charleston,
South Carolina, from 1938 to 1940.

Dottie Chapman and I were married on February 10, 1945.

Our first apartment after we got married was in this house
on Hickman Road in Augusta.

WJBF, my flagship TV station, in Augusta, Georgia.

I enjoyed playing around with the oversized television cameras we used during the early years at WJBF.

Rex, Alan, and I had a good haul when fishing in Fort Lauderdale in September 1960.

PART
II

PRINCIPLES & ADVICE FOR PERSONAL SUCCESS

CHAPTER 5

THE 3 Cs (+1)

Many have described my life as a rags-to-riches story, and in many respects they are right. I truly am an example of the great American dream in which any poor child can achieve great success through courage, determination, hard work, and a little luck.

Raised on a tobacco farm in Virginia where the topsoil was thin and the land was poor, I decided early on that I was not suited for farm life and began preparing myself for a different occupation. My journey toward becoming a multimillionaire started with a little one-tube ham radio that I built myself. Communicating with people all over the world by Morse code from our farmhouse near Prospect, Virginia, opened vast horizons for me.

How this poor farm boy went from there to becoming the head of one of the most successful conglomerates in the country is a real Horatio Alger story. Along the way I built radio and television stations, bought and sold companies like some people bought and sold shares of stock, shaped the careers of some notable politicians, and became close friends with many of the most powerful men in the world.

Everywhere you look, it seems, there are books and people telling you how to get rich quick and make millions of dollars overnight. But there are no shortcuts to really big wealth other than inheriting a bunch of money or winning the lottery. In my experience, I have discovered that there are three important Cs in business: courage, capital, and capacity. These attributes are also applicable to many things in life.

COURAGE

Of the three, courage is the most important, regardless of whether you're in business or some other profession. Courage is what it takes to lead others. Courage is what you do individually, and it is what you will be recognized for. Trust me, you are recognized for what you do individually and not what you do in a group. In all my travels, I have never seen a monument to a committee. There are monuments to generals, not armies. There are monuments to senators, not the Senate. There are schools named after persons. There are roads, streets, and buildings named after individuals, and typically they are named after people who have distinguished themselves because of a great big C: courage.

Along with courage come integrity and honesty, for it takes

courage to maintain these qualities. There are some who think the only way anyone can become successful in business is to take ethical shortcuts. I am proud to say that I have never earned a dishonest penny in my entire business career. Building a reputation as an honest person who always keeps his or her word is as important as establishing a good credit record.

CAPITAL

In business, the C for capital is perhaps the second most important priority. The best way to get capital in business is by using other people's money, and to do that you have to establish good credit and earn credibility with banks, lenders, and the like. I'm going to talk a lot in the next section about how exactly you can go about getting capital when you don't have any to begin with. You don't need to be rich to become richer — you just have to know how to obtain the all-important capital to realize your dreams.

CAPACITY

The third C stands for capacity. It includes not only the skills and knowledge you learn in school, but the continuous curiosity that will follow you all through your life, and your willingness to put in the extra effort. Learning on your own is one of the most powerful ways to increase your capacity, whether it's reading books like I did from the Duke University library or other methods such as listening to audiotapes, attending seminars, or talking to experts in the field. A thirst for more knowledge will give you an edge that will make a huge difference over a period of several years. People who have big capacity think big thoughts and do big things. Sometimes success over the other fellow involves no more than working just two hours a day, ten hours a week longer than he does. In only one year you will have gained 520 hours on him, or three months' more experience and productivity, and in only four years you will have picked up an additional year.

COMMUNICATION

Another important C is communication. It is important not only to communicate your thoughts and ideas to others, but to absorb others' thoughts and ideas as well. There is no substitute for what I call "eyeball-to-eyeball" contact, and there is no type-writer as warm as the human voice. Some of my most success-ful deals came about because I was able to get in my plane and fly anywhere in the country to meet the person I was dealing with face-to-face. Big people make themselves accessible. That means being available for people when they need to talk with you. And I don't mean just physically present — I mean really listening to someone. Paying close attention to what someone is saying when they are talking to you lets them know that what they are saying is important. You not only get more information from people, you also help them build confidence.

In your pursuit of success, it is easy to forget the impor-tance of humility. Humility does not mean never taking credit for your accomplishments; instead, humility is appreciating your abilities while treating others the way you would like to be treated. While it takes self-confidence to make business decisions that involve millions of dollars, too much pride can lead to a downfall. Some of the most successful persons in history have been the most humble.

Everyone has to find his or her own path to success, of course, and this book merely aims to explain how I did it. There is a certain amount of luck involved in any endeavor, but you should never count on it. Most people who appear to have had an unusual amount of luck are usually those who have positioned themselves in order for desirable things to happen to them.

CHAPTER 6

THE 5 RULES

RULE 1: ACT NOW—DON'T DELAY

He who hesitates is lost, as they say, and one of the rules I have always followed in business is "Act now — don't delay." A good example of the value of being decisive — and owning your own plane — is my Martin Theaters deal. In 1969, I began talking to the Martin brothers about buying their company, which included 300 theaters and two television stations in Columbus and Chattanooga.

I was in Pittsburgh when Carl Patrick, the man who actually ran Martin Theaters, called and said that E. D. Martin was in the mood to sell his business. The only thing was that E. D., who had a drinking problem, was leaving for a stint in a rehab hospital the next morning and was likely to change his mind. I told Carl to meet me at the airport in Columbus in an hour and a half and we would see if we could work out something with E. D.

The two brothers and I got together at Carl's house and wrote up an agreement that day on a yellow legal pad for Fuqua Industries to buy their holdings. Shortly after that, Carl called me and said that if I hadn't done the deal right then I never would have gotten the theaters.

Considering we paid $20 million for Martin Theaters and, after some years, sold the two television stations alone for more than $40 million, I'd say that is a powerful example of the importance of seizing the moment in business transactions.

RULE 2: QUALITY VS. QUANTITY

All my businesses have been based on the premise that quality would pay off. More people get rich selling quality than ever got rich selling quantity. That's the reason I made the financial commitment to quality at times when conventional wisdom said I really couldn't afford it. A good example is my decision to "go color" with WJBF-TV. In television, like every other business I was in, I was determined to be first with the best. WJBF had color television in 1954 and, in 1960, it became the second all-color station in Georgia or anywhere in the surrounding area (WSB in Atlanta was first). I bought the first commercial color video equipment when it came on the market. WJBF had all-color operations in the early 1960s when the owners of other stations thought they wouldn't be able to afford it. Eventually the TV station became so profitable it enabled me to expand my business empire into other areas.

RULE 3: CREATE AN ADVANTAGE

One of the things that makes our capitalist system work so well is competition. Being successful often requires that you create an advantage over the other competitors. An advantage can come in many forms. It may be a higher quality or additional service or payment of a larger amount of money or more favorable payment terms. It can also mean the way you communicate your message and the way you deliver it. And, as I demonstrate in the Natco example that follows, it can be very helpful to have an advantage to more effectively communicate your message to employees and other people. Being able to use your advantage at the right time can often be the critical difference in achieving your goal. So, when you're putting together a deal or have something important to communicate, spend some time creating an advantage.

BRUNSWICK CABLE TV DEAL

One of the secrets of success in business is getting in on the ground floor. I had done this with radio and television, and I got into the cable television business in its earliest stages. The first system I built was in Brunswick, Georgia, which served the community of Sea Island. Because Brunswick is located 75 miles from Savannah and 75 miles from Jacksonville, the television signals from stations in those cities were very weak and the demand for better TV reception was great. It was an ideal prospect for a cable system.

I applied to the government of Glynn County for a cable franchise, but they would not give me a franchise for political reasons. I had been dominant in Carl Sanders' campaign for governor, and the political power in Brunswick was on the other side of the fence. A franchise is simply the right to go over and under streets. A group from Columbus had a competing application and was about to get the franchise that I had dropped, but I had another thought. Southern Bell Telephone Co. had a franchise that permitted them to go over and under streets. They had no specific franchise for a cable TV system, but they didn't need one since they had the basic right to use the streets for their telephone franchise. I proposed that Southern Bell build a cable system and lease it to me at a price that would give them a good return and not only accomplish my goal, but would involve my putting up no cash to build a cable system. This had never been done before in the telephone industry, but they agreed to do it.

My cable system was going real well for several years until the FCC decided that telephone companies couldn't use their franchise for telephone service to build a cable television system. I had no investment in the Brunswick cable system, but I sold it for a nice price and that put cash money in my pocket.

Meanwhile, in 1969 I wanted to get the franchise for

cable television in Augusta, but I had what appeared to be serious competition with the City Council. There was another applicant closer to the Council members who was absolutely positive he was going to get the franchise.

When we went to the City Council meeting, both of us proposed giving the city 5 percent of the revenues as a franchise fee. But when they opened my proposal, there was a check for one hundred thousand dollars in advance to show good faith. Needless to say, they gave me the franchise. Our advantage of the six-figure check was our winning edge.

NATCO

In 1965, I gained control of Natco, an old brick-and-tile manufacturer, in order to have a public company. It was the largest company in the industry, even though its sales volume was only about $12 million. The most notable product it had made in its history was the glazed tile that lines the tunnels under the Hudson and East Rivers in New York. It was also the source of the tile used in the Atlanta Police Station at that time.

I wanted to get out of the brick and tile industry, but in the meantime, try to make the company as profitable as possible. Natco had more than a 50 percent share of the brick and tile business in the area in which it competed. It lost money on some contracts, and I knew there must be a way to fix that. One of the problems was that Natco would accept a contract with any colors that an architect could dream up, even though the volume of the particular color might be very small and could be made by any smaller manufacturer.

I called the president of Natco from Augusta and told him I was coming to Pittsburgh to get a better idea of how the business operated. I asked him to get samples of the products Natco made ranked by volume and laid out on the boardroom table so I could see what the business looked like. When I arrived at the office, they had put the samples on the table just as I had asked. To ensure I had the display lined up the way I wanted, I reached across the upper third of the table and wiped off every color below a line drawn with my arm. When the samples clattered to the floor, the expressions on the faces of those old people were ones of absolute shock. They could not believe I had insulted them in that manner.

My purpose, of course, was to determine the relative volume of the various colors. I told them that, beginning immediately, we would make no more of the colors that were on the floor. Those colors we would give to our competitors, who were smaller but who could take small orders and make a profit from them. Natco would no longer produce anything other than about 20 colors. This policy was put into effect and Natco immediately became profitable.

It is remarkable what simple things can be done to change the operating parameters of a business. That dramatic gesture of sweeping the tiles off the table onto the floor was my advantage. I showed them who was in charge and sent a signal that things were going to be done differently. If I had simply called the president and told them to stop making those particular colors, he wouldn't have given me the cooperation he did.

CENTRAL FOUNDRY

Sometimes an advantage is paying more than the market price. A good example is the price I paid to two families for practical control of Central Foundry. I paid considerably above the NYSE quoted market price. Contrary to conventional wisdom, there is no reason that any stockholder cannot sell his stock for any price that he and a buyer agree on. The conventional wisdom says that everybody must get the same price. In this case, I think I paid 25 percent above the price quoted in the paper every day. I have bought control of several public companies by paying above the market for a bloc of stock that included practical management control (not 51 percent) of the public company and made much of my fortune in that manner.

It took several months, but we completed the deal. The end result was that the corporation that owned WJBF was acquired by (merged into) Central Foundry, and I became the dominant and controlling shareholder of Central Foundry. We changed the name from Central Foundry to Gable Industries and the listing remained on the New York Stock Exchange. By initially paying more, I was able to create a new company worth much more.

RULE 4: PAY ATTENTION TO IMPORTANT DETAILS

Details matter. Whether a deal is completed, a sale is made, or a project is finished on time and on budget often comes down to a few critical details. Being organized and making sure the right thing happens at the right time requires time and planning. Whether it requires your getting to the office an hour or two earlier in the morning or staying late, working the details is an important variable in your plan for success.

When you pay attention to details it not only increases your odds for success, it sends a signal to all those you work with and builds their confidence in you. It's an indication that you are taking charge of things, that all is going to work out. That your mutual goal will be achieved. Taking care of the important details creates a foundation of small successes that build a platform for your ultimate success. It also creates a perception of success, which often leads to even greater success.

WINONA WARNER, FORMER SECRETARY FOR FUQUA INDUSTRIES

"Mr. Fuqua is a perfectionist in everything, from his appearance to his business deals. The reason he fired the secretary that I replaced is because she put the carbon paper in backwards for a letter to President Eisenhower. Mr. Fuqua was in the legislature in Atlanta and when he came back home to sign the letter and saw what she had done, that was it. She was gone."

One of the most important ways to be recognized as a success is to dress well. I have been accused of being a clotheshorse, and indeed I do spend a lot of money on my wardrobe. But I never forget that I will have only one chance to make a first impression, and much of that impression will be based on how I am dressed and what I say.

Part of my obsession with being well dressed can be traced back to my childhood. When I was growing up in the country, we didn't have clothes that would take a press and keep it. The first pair of pants I had was blue serge and I literally got up every morning and ironed those pants before I went to school. Every day I would put the iron on the wood stove and heat it so I could press my pants.

Later, when I was working in Charleston as chief engineer of WCSC, I recall walking along the shopping area of King Street when a retired businessman stopped me and said, "Young man, I have been observing you, and you are always well dressed. You will go a long way." His comment caused me to start having my suits tailor-made to the extent that I could afford it. Most people in my earning bracket at that time would have decided they could not afford tailor-made suits, but I had nothing to show but myself and I believed that I could not afford not to have good suits. I had to separate myself from the crowd, and that was one way to do it.

In the 1930s and '40s, there was a chain of clothing stores where men's suits sold for $20 or $25. The stores were called OPO — "One Price Only" — and the suits were better looking than those the average young man bought in regular stores. Sometimes I bought OPO suits, but I always believed in being well dressed to the point of overdoing it. At any given moment, I have more than 20 suits in my closet so that I do not have to wear the same suit more than once every two or three weeks. Every day when I leave home in the morning, I have my housekeeper and my wife check out my appearance. This kind of attention to details has paid off with huge dividends in my lifetime.

RULE 5: DON'T LISTEN TO CONVENTIONAL WISDOM

And, finally, if you want to be a success in business or any field, don't listen to conventional wisdom. If I had paid attention to conventional wisdom, I would not have accomplished one-tenth of the things I did. It is important to think creatively and set high goals. You have to decide if you simply want to lay bricks or build cathedrals.

Remember that big things are done by those who think big.

PART
III

STRATEGIES FOR CREATING GREAT WEALTH

CHAPTER 7

OPM:
THE MOST POWERFUL TOOL

As I mentioned in the previous section during my discussion on capital, using Other People's Money has been very important in my business dealings. If you learn to borrow money and develop a credit reputation, you can get other people's money to work for you.

GETTING STARTED

At an early age, even as a teenager, I learned that having credit would be essential in a business career. Little things such as borrowing against my savings passbook helped establish my reputation. Later, as I mentioned, I bought real estate lots and borrowed the money to build houses on them. When I sold each house, I would repay the loan and use the profits to repeat the process until I had established a good relationship with the banks.

Never forget that you'll never get rich if you don't use Other People's Money, and that's all a mortgage is. In fact, I can demonstrate in many instances when it is smart to put a mortgage on one's home and invest the money in something that will give a larger return than the cost of the interest on the mortgage.

MY FIRST DEALS

Very early in my career, I wanted to build a radio station. As I mentioned earlier, I made a business plan for three cities and finally settled upon Augusta, Georgia. I had the whole thing figured out: which city to target, how to build and market a new station there, a fully integrated vision for success. All I needed was the money. If I could get someone to put up the $10,000 it would take to build the radio station, I knew I could make it profitable.

I didn't know a soul in Augusta, but I was determined to make it happen. Fortunately for me, Lester Moody was the first person I met, and he believed in me enough to help me get financing. Within a single day, he found three investors who were willing to take a chance on me. My whole career began thanks to my making good use of other people's money.

In 1949, I was finally able to afford to buy outright a radio station of my own, WTNT. Although I had done well for myself, I still needed other people's money to make this big purchase happen. Fortunately I had had the vision and business sense to realize a big moment when it presented itself. I had learned several years before that the Royal Crown Bottling Company could be bought because of an "unwarranted surplus" tax problem. My friend Fred Kennedy and I had seized the opportunity immediately. I agreed to pay the owner $125,000 for the business, and since this price was about the same amount as the cash the owner had accumulated through unpaid dividends, I basically used this accumulated cash to buy the business — I put up no money of my own.

When I decided a few years later that I wanted out of Royal Crown, I sold my half-interest to Kennedy for $100,000. Remember, I had put up not one cent of my own money in the whole endeavor. But with that $100,000, I was finally able to buy my own radio station.

CLAUSSENS BAKERY DEAL

By 1963, my reputation as an astute businessman had grown to the point that a group of local businessmen approached me about buying Claussens Bakery. Unfortunately, I jumped at the chance before carefully examining the situation.

At first glance, it looked like a good deal. Claussens was doing $12 million a year in business. Claussens Bakery had been owned by a German family who came to this country in the early 1800s, and they had established bakeries in Columbia, Charleston, and Greenville. They were doing quite well until they decided to get out of the business and sell the company to the public.

Things had not gone smoothly after that. The management was not very capable, and the directors wanted to sell and get the stockholders out of the business. I made them a proposition in which I would give them a note for each stockholder for two dollars a share, or whatever the market was at the time. The note would be due in 20 years at 6 percent interest. It would be unsecured and my television station, WJBF, would own the bakery. The only security was the value of the note, which was backed up by the television station and the bakery. As a result, I paid $946,000 for the company without putting in a nickel of my own money. This was Other People's Money at work. Imagine buying a $12 million bakery for only $946,000!

So here I was in the bakery business and I knew nothing about it. I put young Tom Hennessy in charge and we ended up spending a lot of money on equipment without making any profits. That wasn't so bad, however, because the television station made so much money the bakery's losses could be written off against WJBF's earnings.

My mistake was not realizing how obsolete the equipment was and how expensive it would be to bring it up to date. The other factor was the crazy way the bakery industry operated. You brought in the bread to a grocery store one day and, if it didn't sell, you picked it up the next day and left fresh loaves. I promised myself never again to get into a business that sold a product with only a 24-hour shelf life.

GEORGIA POWER BUILDING

There were other opportunities to use Other People's Money in my business dealings. I built a million-dollar building in Augusta for Georgia Power without putting a nickel of my own money into it. The deal was, Georgia Power didn't want to put the building on their books. I built it for them with a mortgage from an insurance company and the rent they paid was the exact amount it took to pay the mortgage each month.

This had tax advantages as well because the depreciation can be written off every year. Eventually the mortgage gets paid off and the building is free and clear. This is the kind of thing most anybody can do. They just have to seek out the opportunities and use the tax code to their advantage. There's nothing illegal about it.

KENTUCKY COAL MINE

Another good example of using Other People's Money is the deal Rex and I made for a coal mine in Pikeville, Kentucky, the site of the famous Hatfield and McCoy feud. We had been doing well in the oil and gas business, but we were looking for an opportunity to further capitalize on the rising prices of energy by getting into the coal business.

The strip mine that was for sale was owned by two young men who had a cost-plus contract with a utility company. All they had to do was put the coal in railroad cars and ship it to power plants and bill the utility company what it cost to mine the coal plus a generous profit in addition. The power company paid every expense, and such a contract was highly profitable since it required a moderate investment in mining equipment and a minimum in labor. These sweetheart contracts were common in the utility industry in the 1970s.

REX FUQUA

"This deal was interesting because the characters involved were so unusual. These fellows we bought the business from were miners who were born and bred in hardscrabble Kentucky. They never thought they'd make so much money. They were equipment operators who ended up signing a long-term contract with the power company and suddenly they were making a lot of money and couldn't wait to cash out and go buy cars and houses. We arrived in Pikeville, Kentucky, and the fellow had an office on the second floor of this nondescript little building. He had the largest hands I ever saw. They were the size of baseball mitts. It was fun to negotiate with these guys because they were smart. They were uneducated, but they were smart. All of the people there were laughing at these people with suits coming up there to buy a coal mine."

The mine was another unwarranted surplus situation much like my first capital buy, the Royal Crown Bottling Co.

The two miners who owned it had accumulated so much cash that they were about to be penalized for not paying dividends. The dividends, of course, would have been subject to ordinary income tax rates. They wanted to sell the company and have capital gains treatment on their profits rather than the income tax rate. The value was in the contract. There wasn't much to the mining operation.

We offered them $4.5 million for the whole thing. Two and a half million was to be paid in cash, which we would take out of their bank account. Two million was to be paid over a period of several years, based on the profits that could be projected precisely under the terms of the power company contract. We picked up a contract worth many millions without spending as much as a postage stamp as all the funds we needed came right out of the miners' bank accounts. They, incidentally, went into business the next day in another mining project.

Several years later, a man showed up at Rex's office in Atlanta saying he wanted to buy the coal mine from us. The proposition was that he would give us $5 million in cash and we would give him the coal mining business including the all-important utility contract. Thus, we picked up $5 million in cash without ever having made a penny of investment. A basic understanding of taxes is fundamental of seizing opportunities such as this.

CHAPTER 8

LEVERAGE: MAKING THE MOST OF YOUR RESOURCES

Leverage is investing only a small percentage of your own money into a financial project that effectively yields a high rate of return for your investment because someone else has put up the remaining money. Very similar to one of my favorite concepts, Using Other People's Money. With leverage, you're putting some of your money in with other people's money. You both are putting money on the line, risking capital for potential. This can take several forms. One way that we're all familiar with is a mortgage. When you buy a $300,000 house and put 20 percent down ($60,000), the mortgage company matches your money with a $240,000 loan to you. If you sell the house five years later for $400,000, you've made a profit of $100,000. But you didn't have to put all the $300,000 up to realize this gain. You've leveraged your $60,000 for the gain in market value of your property.

PLAYING THE YIELD CURVE

In the early 1990s interest rates were declining steadily. Long-term government bonds a few years earlier went as high as 20 percent, when the normal rate on this type of bond historically is about 5 percent. If one believed that interest rates would continue to decline, there were two ways to make a profit. One way was to buy long-term (30-year) government bonds and hold them as they increased in value as interest rates declined. This is the ultimate in safety in bond investment. But the ultimate in profit is to be made by buying the bonds with funds borrowed at a lower rate than the bonds paid. This is called playing the yield curve.

I made big money by borrowing at the federal funds rate, which varies from day to day, and buying government bonds. During this period of declining interest rates, I typically borrowed at 3 percent and bought bonds at 8 percent to 9 percent. This is done through the repo market, which you shouldn't mess with without a good broker. I typically would buy $10 million worth of bonds that were selling at, say, 8 percent. I borrowed $9 million at, say, 3 percent. Obviously, I had the income from the bonds at an annualized rate of 8 percent or $800,000, which cost me 3 percent or $300,000 annualized. The amount of risk can be considered to vary based upon how much leverage one is willing to operate with. Ten percent is a typical trader's leverage basis. Actually, at that time it was possible to borrow 98 percent of the face value of the 30-year bonds, meaning you could buy $100 million of bonds for $2 million cash. I did that on a few occasions and luckily the interest rate spread usually went my way, but it's very risky unless one is an expert in bond trading.

INSURANCE BUSINESS

I was always fascinated by what appeared to be unusual opportunities in the life insurance business, which is the ultimate in the art of using other people's money. In life insurance, the companies take in the premiums and get the use of the money, usually for many years, before the insured person dies and the company has to pay.

It takes only a small amount of capital to provide leverage for a life insurance company. A group of us, including Carl Sanders, who later became governor of Georgia, and Ernest "Fritz" Hollings, who became governor of South Carolina and later a U.S. senator, got together $300,000 to start U.S. Guaranty Life Insurance Company. I was the largest stockholder and, in those days, $300,000 allowed us to have a life insurance company that was well financed. Also, the "U.S." gave it a sort of authenticity that helped our salesmen sell life insurance policies.

We operated U.S. Guaranty for a few years and then merged it into another insurance company, that in turn was later merged into another company. We came out quite well on our investment.

I had studied the life insurance business until I understood what it took to build that kind of company. We not only developed the know-how, but we employed experienced management people, which made the whole idea a successful venture. Because I had studied the business, I talked a good game and my partners deferred major decisions to me. I have been in several situations of this kind with my private activities, and I always was conscious of the fact I was using somebody else's money. In order to protect my own investment, I had to protect the investments of others.

The leverage factor in insurance is so attractive. This is the ability to develop a large operation with a minimum amount of capital and the use of Other People's Money. If I had my business career to do over, I think I would have built a large insurance company to be the parent of the other companies I was buying and selling.

ALMOND ORCHARD

If you remember the 3 Cs, a fair number of opportunities will come to your attention if you have developed a good reputation for making prompt decisions. Here is a good example of using leverage that came to Rex and me in the late 1980s. The Bank of America was cleaning out its bad loan closet. Rex was living in San Francisco and never let the Bank of America forget that we had money and would act quickly if they had a deal we might be interested in. Bank of America had gone through a period when they had made a huge volume of agricultural loans. They had foreclosed on a twenty-six-hundred-acre almond grove, and we negotiated to buy it for a down payment of $1.5 million. After a few years we decided to take our profit. We sold it to an Indian immigrant for $12 million cash. So we leveraged our relatively small initial investment to a sales value of significantly more. The property had a replacement cost of close to $25 million. Our internal rate of return was quite good. My policy has been to take a good profit when it is available and not be greedy.

CHAPTER 9

OPB:
USING OTHER PEOPLE'S BRAINS

Hiring competent people with good character is one of the keys to a company's success. If you're going to grow a company and build wealth, it's very difficult to do it alone. Building a team of strong people that put their brains to work behind you is kind of knowledge leverage. It's your job to create the climate, provide the resources, and create the communication and vision of where the company should go. Then all that "brain power" can be focused on achieving the goals of what you want to accomplish.

Many times, rather than grow a business from scratch, I would go after a business whose management I admired. I know one of the things I'm buying when I take over a company is all the brains that have made it successful. The theory of the con-glomerates, which I believed then and now, is that it is cheaper to buy a business than it is to develop one. And it is wiser to buy a company with a good management base in place than to come in and try to fix something that isn't broken.

A good example of the difference between growing a business and buying one that is already established with the management in place was Fuqua Industries' purchase of Georgia Federal Savings and Loan Co. in 1984. This was a $2.5 billion institution that we got into and out of with a sizable profit. If we had started a new savings and loan, it would have taken all of my lifetime to develop what Georgia Federal had in assets. The same can apply to almost any business. It takes time to gain market share and acceptance and to develop the all-important management for a successful business. It is simply cheaper to buy a going business with an established product and a history of competent management.

Sometimes I did supplement existing management with additional expertise. Even though I knew Georgia Federal was a well-run company, I thought it was important to bring on seasoned banking professional Dick Jackson as president and CEO after I bought it. Our goal in this case was to expand Georgia Federal's business out of traditional savings and loan and retail bank accounts into small-company and middle-market banking relationships. And I knew that Jackson would be the perfect man for the job. Georgia Federal chairman John Zellars wasn't enthusiastic about my taking over the bank, but after a few months he liked the changes he saw and decided I was a pretty good fellow. He and I became good friends. The point is, I knew I had a good base to start with. Bringing in Jackson was, I hoped, going to be the icing on the cake. And I was right.

RICHARD JACKSON

"I think J. B. has an uncanny ability to evaluate the financial side of a company. He could really pick out companies that were reliable. And he hired good people, paid them extremely well, and gave them good upside growth bonus opportunities as well as stock options. Also, he always had somebody who was a really bright guy who could keep all the pieces together while he looked at the big picture. When he bought Georgia Federal, he thought it was going to give him a certain respectability in the market that he didn't have at that time. He had no idea the changes that were going to take place in the S&L industry, and neither did I, but the bank made him a lot of money."

Probably my best example of using other people's brains was my decision early in my career to hire Tom Hennessy at WFAK in Charleston. He was only about 17 years old then, but I recognized from the start that he had a lot of ability and energy. It was one of the best hiring decisions I ever made, for Tom lived up to my expectations and he increasingly moved into responsible jobs with me as I acquired other businesses over the years.

I could depend on Tom to use his judgment in handling

any job. When I acquired the Claussens Bakery, I put Tom in charge of the operation, even though his previous experience had been in radio and television. In the early years at WJBF-TV, he worked a variety of jobs, from station manager to on-air announcer. His versatility was a great help to me.

TOM HENNESSY

"J. B. was like a father to me, but I can count on the fingers of one hand the times he ever called me in his office and said, 'Tom, you really did a good job on that project or assignment.' He would make you understand that you did all right, but that you could have done better. He set high standards for himself, and he expected everyone to have the same high standards. He was smart enough to hire self-motivating people. That's what helped create success for him."

As I've mentioned, I always tried to find companies that had good management in place, and I used those managers' brains to good advantage. When I bought Martin Theaters, I realized that Carl Patrick knew more about the company than anyone. Carl did such a good job that I later made him president and chief operating officer of Fuqua Industries.

The Trojan Seed Company is another example of a

company that was run by some savvy managers. When we acquired it, we provided the capital they needed, and they provided the brain power. Trojan's executives had developed a shrewd marketing plan in which they recruited the most successful farmers in each county to be farmer/dealers of their seed product. We liked the initiative this demonstrated, and we were not about to change the way they were successfully running the company.

Let me emphasize that there is a lot of difference between management ability and management ambition. We all see a lot of companies with capable top management, and we frequently find able management at all levels within a given company. It is quite another thing to possess both the management talent and the ambition to make a business grow.

One manager who possessed both talent and ambition was Nelson Strawbridge. When we acquired the photofinisher Colorcraft in 1966, we kept Strawbridge, who was the company's founder, in place to run it for us. He continued to make acquisitions and he set high goals for himself. When he told us that a proposed acquisition would grow at a rate of 15 percent a year, he always delivered.

Larry Klamon was another bright young man whom I hired to run Fuqua Industries. He was educated as a lawyer at Yale University and he quickly learned what I expected in a manager.

LARRY KLAMON

"When J. B. is confident in people and thinks they know what they're doing, he gives them tremendous amounts of responsibility. I used to give him acquisitions proposals and he would read them over and ask me why we were doing this. After a while, when he became convinced that I knew what I was doing, I would come in with a 50-page document that involved millions of dollars and he would say, 'Does this look OK to you?' and I would say 'Yes' and he would sign it. J. B. did use Other People's Brains, but he also used his own."

In my long career, I have learned that the most successful business people are those who hire employees who are experts in some field. Otherwise, you'll spin your wheels worrying about details instead of focusing on the big picture.

CHAPTER 10

FINANCIAL STRATEGIES

ARBITRAGE TRADING

One of the ways in which I made substantial profits is through arbitrage stock trading. This can be very complicated or it can be very simple. The simplest way to do arbitrage is to buy the stock of a company that has announced it is being acquired by another company and pay a price higher than the quoted price of the company to be acquired. You wait for the deal to close and then sell the stock and take a profit. In the simplest situation, Bank A announces an offer to buy Bank B on a share-for-share basis. Bank A stock is selling for $50 a share, and Bank B is selling for $45 a share. Buy Bank B and, assuming there is no change in the price of Bank A and assuming that it takes six months to go through the regulatory process to close the deal, there is a profit of $5 a share if you hold Bank B stock until the deal closes. This is a gross profit of slightly more than 10 percent, which is nothing to get excited about, except that you get the 10 percent in six months, which is 20 percent annualized. I use banks as an example, but regular corporations' mergers usually close in less than six months.

Simple arbitrage is something that can be done by any experienced investor without a lot of risk. It has even less risk if you can eliminate the effect of the market prices on both Bank A and Bank B between the time of the announcement and the time of close, but that is more complicated. One way to do this is to buy the stock of Bank B and sell short the stock of Bank A. This would lock in a price differential of $5 that would not change, regardless of how the stocks of the individual banks perform between the announcement of the acquisition and the close. At the close, you tender your shares of Bank A that you will acquire from selling the shares of Bank B, which was your original deal.

I have made a lot of money through the years by doing simple arbitrage. For example, when it became apparent that Ross Johnson was going to put RJ Reynolds up for sale, I bought a substantial number of shares (for me) at about $75. As the bidding rose, I sold out at about $110 per share, and the bidding process did not take but a few weeks, so my annualized profit rate was indeed exciting. If you are going to do any type of stock trading, other than simple buying and selling, I would advise using a broker who is experienced in the more complicated types of transactions.

Another simple trading practice that I engaged in for a year or two was having a good broker who observed the news section of his computer monitor so that he could catch everything when it was announced. There was, for a much longer period of time than I can explain, a simple scheme whereby you could buy the stock of any company when it announced that it might be added to the S&P 500 Index. There is a steady stream of companies being added to the S&P 500 as companies drop out because of mergers, change of trading markets, etc., and these stocks must be replaced by other companies. When the announcement of an addition to the S&P 500 is made, it will give a date on which the transaction will take place, usually about a week away. The trade is to buy on the announcement and sell on the transaction (listing) date. Depending on volatility of the market as a whole, you will lose on some of these deals, but you will gain a small amount on most of them. Since your money is invested for only a few days, the annualized gain, if any, will be substantial. I no longer do this because so many people began doing it that the profit margins became too small for the risk involved.

You need a good broker if you are going to do anything in the stock market other than simply buying and selling of shares of stock. In fact, sometimes it's good practice to have more than one, especially if you are someone who adjusts their portfolio frequently. I currently have three brokers, Ron Hart, Taylor Glover, and Ted Macuch, and, although each primarily fills a different investment need for me, I can always track down at least one of the three at any time to answer whatever question I might have. I do not have the inclination or time to research stocks and to make judgments that are profitable. I do the commonsense things. I never owned a single share of what we call "dot.com" stock. I couldn't understand them and I don't invest in anything that I don't understand. I felt that dot.coms really meant "dot.com, dot.go."

STRUCTURING BALANCE SHEETS

My expertise in management was not in the details of administration, but rather in the efforts at increasing value. If I was a significant stockholder in a company for which I was responsible, I had a double incentive to see that the value of the company's stock increased. I was at my best in structuring balance sheets. Most successful managers are probably those who work on the operating side of the financials. I believe in managing the balance sheet. Financial strategy is the essence of the entrepreneur's game.

When I see a company that has no debt or has a low ratio of debt to equity, I am not impressed. Under our tax system, the IRS gets on average about 40 percent of the profits at the corporate level. If there is debt in the capital structure, that level of taxation can be directly offset by the ability to treat interest as a tax-deductible expense. If I were constructing a balance sheet for a corporation, a partnership or individual, I would set up the capital structure at 50 percent debt and 50 percent equity. A simple calculation would show that the return on equity would be significantly higher under this structure than if the debt were only a small part of the capital. The debt itself may be leveraged, and this is a point that many managers overlook. It is the type of debt, as well as debt itself, that makes the difference. Banks, insurance companies, and other institutional lenders treat subordinated debt as equity. If subordinated debt is a part of capital for borrowing purposes, it is the equivalent of added equity of common and/or preferred stock. I have never understood why many balance sheets include preferred stock when the preferred dividend is taxable at ordinary rates, again about 40 percent, and is not deductible as an expense. Surely, it is better to have subordinated debt than it is to have preferred stock.

I look at capital as the raw material in any business. It makes sense to me to try to obtain this raw material at the cheapest possible price. When I can deduct the interest of debt as an expense, it is certainly the cheaper way to go and enables, theoretically, almost infinite leverage of the common equity. The common stockholder deserves to have a higher reward than a lender to compensate for the higher risk inherent in common stock. At Fuqua Industries this kind of thinking about the capital structure was how I operated, and it was the type of structure I attempted to influence with companies in which I had a lesser influence than Fuqua Industries.

I do not believe in paying dividends under our income tax structure. If the stockholder is paid a dividend, it can only come after taxes have been paid on corporate earnings, which will be 50 percent. The income tax that the stockholder pays will be another 40 percent or 50 percent of the net spendable income he receives. If a stockholder needs income, it makes a lot more sense for him to sell some of his shares in a public company and pay the 20 percent capital gains tax (if applicable) instead of taking a dividend on which he has to pay a tax of more than twice as much as the capital gains rate. Of course, these tax examples apply only if we are referring to a profitable business.

PART
IV

A LIFE FULL OF DEALS

CHAPTER 11

THE BEGINNINGS OF FUQUA INDUSTRIES

NATCO

I had developed substantial capital from the TV station and my other businesses through the 1950s and early 1960s when I saw all these fellows from the Young Presidents Organization (YPO) running public companies. I thought, well, that's the way you leverage your money.

I had been a member of the YPO since about 1953. The YPO is an organization of young men and women who have become presidents or chief executive officers of their companies by age 35. As I got to know more people in YPO, I learned that most of them were heads of publicly owned companies. I was fascinated by the apparent difference between operating a private company, as I had been doing, and operating a company owned by shareholders.

I decided to look for an opportunity to be the head of a public company while at the same time keeping the benefits of the autonomy of a private company. My approach to getting into a public company was to buy control of a company with a listing on the stock exchange and then use this as a vehicle to swap stock for other companies and thus build a conglomerate. This was in the 1960s when the conglomerate era was beginning to peak. A conglomerate is nothing more than a group of unrelated companies that may produce everything from shoestrings to food products.

I read hundreds of annual reports looking for just the kind of vehicle I wanted. One that interested me was Great Lakes Industries, a small over-the-counter (OTC) company that had a plating business in California and a principal business making stoneware in a plant in Illinois. The interesting thing about this was that Great Lakes Industries also owned 25 percent of Natco, a brick and tile manufacturer that had a listing on the New York Stock Exchange. Looking at the directors of both companies, I saw that Great Lakes controlled Natco. I approached a lawyer in Philadelphia who was listed on the proxies of both companies and who in effect would be the obvious person to contact in connection with Great Lakes Industries. This man said that my interest was timely because he and his partners, who had only recently gained control of Natco through a proxy fight, had decided they would like to liquidate their investment.

We arrive at a complicated transaction. To get to Natco, I had to buy the stock of Great Lakes Industries that was owned by the partnership that controlled both companies. Then I had to offer the other shareholders of Great Lakes Industries the same consideration. That would give me control of Great Lakes Industries. Part of the agreement was that these directors would resign from the board of Natco and elect my nominees in their places. This process would give me control of the company.

I was able to get together enough cash to buy out the stockholders of Great Lakes Industries, but there was one snag: these people had personally guaranteed Natco's note for $3 million at the Pennsylvania National Bank, and they naturally wanted to be relieved of their endorsement. After persuading the First National Bank in Atlanta to take over the $3 million note with my endorsement, I was halfway to my goal. Next we had a meeting in Pittsburgh, where Natco was located and where the change in directors was to take place. Great Lakes Industries only had five of the nine directors of Natco, and there was hostility between the two groups, so it was not a simple matter of bringing my people on as the Great Lakes directors came off.

Some friends in Augusta agreed to be directors and came to Pittsburgh for the event. We planned to swap in my people as each of the five Great Lakes directors resigned. We did this by having the Great Lakes majority pass a resolution to add a director to the Natco board. Then they nominated one of my directors. We then went around the table and each Great Lakes director resigned so that my people could be seated.

The hostility between the two groups was something

new to me. I always thought I could work with anybody if given a reasonable chance. To avoid a continuation of this adversarial relationship on my board, I picked out two of the old Natco directors and attempted to convince them that I was a decent person and that they should not fight me. Persuading them was no easy task, but eventually they became the strongest supporters I ever had on any board. After I had given them my special treatment, I could do no wrong as far as they were concerned.

After that, I made myself chairman and began to do what I had planned to do in the way of public companies. The first thing I had to deal with was the company's management. Natco was headquartered in Pittsburgh above the Lane Bryant store. It had file cabinets going back for decades, it had no officers under the age of 65, and it had no pension plan. I was not about to turn out all of those old people without some consideration. Those who needed to be retired with some benefits were taken care of by my reaching into my pocket and paying them myself. This continued for some of them for years.

My next object, as I discussed earlier in the book, was to make Natco more profitable. After I established (through that unconventional tile demonstration) that Natco would only continue to produce the top 20 colors of tile, the company immediately began making money.

The Natco deal closed on September 30, 1965. At the beginning of 1966 we changed the name to Fuqua Industries and put my name in the newspaper stock listings every day. It enabled me to develop a personal image that was desirable and demonstrated that I had enough confidence in the companies I had accumulated to put my own name on the door. This is rarely done anymore, but I think it requires restudying. There is a certain value in the head of a business having his or her name as part of the company identity.

POLARIS

The most important deal I ever made is the one I negotiated shortly after acquiring Natco. I was in my hotel room in New York when John Stebbins, a radio and television broker, called me about a business opportunity. Stebbins knew that I had this new company and that I might be a prospect for another television station. He said that the only VHF television station in Evansville, Indiana, was for sale by the Polaris Corporation, which was headquartered in Milwaukee. I personally owned radio station WROZ (Rosy Radio) in Evansville already. Polaris was a corporation that had been created to enable a Milwaukee bank to get involved in a plan of urban renewal in the city's downtown area.

This company was the number-one bank in Milwaukee, but at that time no national bank could own buildings and property not devoted to the banking business. Therefore, it was unable to construct new office buildings for rent or do any other kind of urban renewal.

The bank found a clever way around this rule, however. They contracted to build the biggest office building in Milwaukee in the name of a newly created corporation called

Polaris. The stock of Polaris was spun out from the bank to the bank's stockholders. So all of the building and downtown improvements were done by Polaris and not the bank — and thus the banking laws of the time were circumvented.

The people at the bank turned over the development of Polaris to a very colorful individual who thought, as I did, that the era of conglomerates was upon us. He bought everything that was for sale, including some warehouses and the television station in Evansville; an island in Mobile Bay, Alabama; television stations in Fargo, North Dakota, and Winnipeg, Canada; radio stations here and there; and a taxicab company. It was really an odd assortment of businesses, and getting involved with Polaris could prove to be opening a can of worms. But it was an opportunity that exceeded my dreams because I saw the possibility of getting the Evansville television station and the other stations through a different route.

The reason Polaris had not sold the television station to date was because the bank wanted to do a deal where the Polaris stockholders, who were also stockholders in the bank, would not have to pay any taxes. The way to do this was through some type of stock deal for the whole of Polaris. Others who had looked at the possibility of buying the TV stations were not interested in going that route because they could not determine the real value of the assets of Polaris.

My plan was to exchange Natco stock for the Polaris stock so the Polaris stockholders would end up with a listing on the New York Stock Exchange and no taxes to pay. I would then pick out the TV stations and liquidate the rest of the assets, leaving me with just TV and radio stations in Natco.

Stebbins arranged for me to meet with the top man at Polaris the next morning and by the end of breakfast, we had worked out a deal in which I gave convertible preferred stock in exchange for Polaris common stock. The deal was done without any complications and I ended up with all of the conglomerate's assets. Now the bank management could tell its shareholders they had given them stock that was marketable, that paid them dividends, and that was likely to be a great success in view of the plan to develop a conglomerate, which was in fashion in the 1960s. This was a great story and the bank's stockholders embraced it with much enthusiasm.

As I said, nobody else had tried to do this because they had no idea what the assets of Polaris were worth. There were large mortgages against office buildings and other properties the organization owned and it was impossible to determine if there was any value in the properties over the mortgages. But this deal was so important to me that I was willing to take a chance that the properties mortgaged were worth at least as much as the mortgage. Otherwise, they probably would not have been able to get the loan. It seemed a rather simple conclusion, and one that was proven correct when I began liquidating the properties.

Now, what this did for me was to give me all of the assets, including the television station, that Polaris had already accumulated. It gave me a big start in my plan to develop a conglomerate. This was the neatest solution to the public relations problem of the bank and to the practical problem I had as the new boy on the block. When I look back on my career, I view this transaction to be perhaps the most important one among the many companies I bought and sold. From a purely financial standpoint, the acquisition of Polaris was probably the best deal I ever made.

MARTIN THEATERS

Not long after I acquired Natco, I began talking to the Martin brothers about buying their company of 300 movie theaters and television stations in Columbus and Chattanooga. The two brothers owned the company, but a fellow named Carl Patrick actually ran it.

CARL PATRICK

"J. B. and I had become friends after we did the WJBF deal, and my wife and I used to go to dinner with him and Dottie. One day he sent me a letter asking me to look over this theater company he was thinking about buying and tell him what I thought it was worth.

"Well, at the time the Martin brothers had tremendous estate tax problems and we wanted to sell the company. Back then $20 million was a lot of money, and we figured that's what we would get for the business. So I called him and said, 'J. B., why don't you buy Martin Theaters?' He said, 'Pat, are you kidding me?' I said, 'No, I'm serious,' so he flew down from Pittsburgh and met me in Columbus and we worked out the deal. That was in 1969 and I was allowed to stay on and operate Martin Theaters with complete autonomy."

Martin Theaters were primarily in smaller communities in the South and Southwest. Their assets also included many drive-in theaters, which were beginning to lose their popularity at that time. The beautiful thing about this was, as drive-ins were going out of style, shopping centers were being built. The land it took to hold a drive-in theater in many cases became valuable real estate for shopping malls, since most of the drive-ins were on the outskirts of larger cities. And with the Martin Theater Co. also came two highly profitable television stations in Columbus and Chattanooga, Tennessee.

Altogether, Martin Theaters was one of the best acquisitions Fuqua Industries ever made. We paid $20 million for the theater company and after some years we sold the two television stations alone for more than $40 million. We later sold Martin Theaters to Carl Patrick, who had managed the company before we bought it. I foresaw the need for substantial additional capital to build multiscreen theaters with the prospect of little growth in the industry. Subsequently, almost all of these theater chains have gone into bankruptcy because their expansions to multiscreen theaters took more of their capital than they could get back in a reasonable period.

Carl Patrick bought the theaters from Fuqua in a leveraged buyout and, together with his sons, greatly expanded the investment under the name Carmike Theaters.

COLORCRAFT

One of our earliest acquisitions was Colorcraft, a small wholesale photofinisher that had annual revenues of less than $3 million when we bought it in 1966. Nelson Strawbridge, who was the founder of the company, built it up to about $350 million over the next 20 years.

The enthusiasm of Nelson Strawbridge was like that of few people I had known. He continued to run the company and make dozens of acquisitions of smaller photofinishing companies. Strawbridge, who had an earn-out for five years after we acquired Colorcraft, became a multimillionaire and was well rewarded for his efforts. When he came in with a proposed acquisition, he uniformly predicted that it would grow at a rate of 15 percent per year. Strawbridge delivered in practically all cases.

LARRY KLAMON, FORMER CEO OF FUQUA INDUSTRIES

"The companies that were the most successful, and certainly Colorcraft was one of them, were those in which the people who were there when we bought them stayed until retirement and built the companies. At one point we had

21 millionaires working for Fuqua Industries. These were people who could have just bagged it and they didn't. One of the attractions was the fact that we handled all the financing and provided the resources that allowed them to do their thing. With Colorcraft, the whole industry was consolidating, and with our support Colorcraft bought 20 or 30 companies and expanded like an amoeba all across the country. They couldn't have done that on their own because they wouldn't have had the resources."

Colorcraft continually invested in machinery and equipment that enabled it to be the low-cost producer. As it expanded its territory, Colorcraft successfully negotiated contracts for photofinishing services with America's largest retailers, such as K-mart and many of the drugstore and grocery chains. For the retailer, this service was profitable because the photofinishing service occupied very little floor space and required no investment in inventory. Retail customers would come in, leave their film at the counter, and come back the following day to pick up the processed film. Colorcraft's courier would stop by the store each day to pick up the film and bring back the prints the next day.

In 1987, Fox Photo became available for acquisition, but we were outbid by Eastman Kodak. We then went to Eastman Kodak and offered to sell them Colorcraft, which they refused.

Eventually, however, Kodak came back to us and asked if we would be interested in forming a joint venture corporation that would own both Colorcraft and the Kodak processing businesses. After extensive negotiations, the joint venture, named Qualex, was formed with Fuqua Industries owning 51 percent.

We made an agreement when Qualex was created that if there was a change of control at Fuqua Industries, Kodak would have a right to increase its ownership to 50 percent from 49 percent, and thus have the right to veto any dividends to be paid. After Charles "Red" Scott acquired the controlling shares in Fuqua Industries, Eastman Kodak elected to exercise this right. When I sold out and left Fuqua Industries in 1989, we had by far the largest photofinishing business in the world with sales of around $700 million.

SNAPPER COMPANY

Our most successful acquisitions have been the companies being run by entrepreneurs who had a genuine interest in developing their business, but who needed a source of capital to maintain the growth rate. By far the best business Fuqua Industries ever acquired was Snapper Power Equipment Company, which manufactured lawn and garden equipment. Headquartered in McDonough, Georgia, the company was originally called McDonough Power Equipment, Inc.

In 1967, I was contacted by a business broker in Atlanta who wanted to know if I would like to own the Snapper lawn mower business. Having a policy of never turning down an opportunity, I agreed to let him take me to see the owners of this enterprise. In McDonough, we met Bill Smith, who was the president of this little manufacturing company that had annual sales of about $10 million. He pretended that his business was not for sale, but he allowed me to make a presentation of what my vision was for Fuqua Industries and how valuable the stock would be in the future. Of course, I emphasized that if he intended to keep expanding, he would need capital that we could supply. As Smith became more interested, I told the broker that he should go back to Atlanta and let us talk; I would find some way to get back to the airport myself.

Smith and I worked out a stock deal where part of the stock would be paid initially and the rest paid over a five-year period, based on growth of earnings. Both the business and the price of Fuqua Industries stock did so well over the five-year period that all three of the founders of McDonough Power Equipment Company became multimillionaires.

Bill Smith was one of the best operating executives I have ever met. He had an understanding of marketing, research and development, accounting and finance, organization and motivation of individuals. It was under Smith's leadership that Snapper had developed a premium quality product. Among the company's innovations were the efficient rear engine riding mower and the placement of the bag between the handles of a push mower, which allowed it to get close to a fence or tree on either side.

Snapper also had a two-step distribution system with more than 100 distributors and almost 10,000 dealers. Anthony "Tony" Malizia, who had a minority financial interest in Snapper when it was sold to us, had developed this network. He knew all the distributors and their families, and attended their weddings and major events as though they were one big family. The distributors had protected territories and they sold the products to dealers who had exclusive sales rights over defined areas. The Snapper lawn mower was the highest quality product in its industry and its price was the highest, too.

With an emphasis on quality rather than on quantity, Snapper could get a price on its products that ensured everyone would earn a good profit. The distributor made 20 percent and the dealer, having a protected sales territory and a premium-priced product, also did very well. Thus, everybody in the distribution chain — the manufacturer, the distributor, and the dealer — all prospered.

In the dozen years since we acquired the company, sales had grown from $10 million to $250 million, and profits increased accordingly. Smith, one of the original founders, retired in due course and was succeeded by his partner, "Tony" Malizia.

LARRY KLAMON

"I remember being in Italy and taking a tour of the Vatican and I saw that they had a Snapper riding lawn mower. They were kidding Tony Malizia, an Italian-Catholic whose policy on exports was that you had to pay for it before it left the dock. The distributor called up and said, 'Tony, I understand your policy, but don't you think the Vatican is good for it?' So Tony made an exception for the Pope."

In the late '80s, we were spending $25 million per year on advertising and marketing for Snapper. We had a plan whereby we would match — to an unlimited amount — whatever dollars the dealer and/or the distributor wanted to put into advertising. That policy paid off handsomely and was self-controlling because no dealer would pay more for advertising than he could afford.

When I sold out my interest in Fuqua Industries in 1989, my successor, Charles "Red" Scott, had no experience in a consumer products business. He immediately began a program of eliminating the distributors on the theory that he could sell his product to the Wal-Marts and Home Depots and avoid paying the 20 percent to the distributor. This was an almost fatal mistake. These mass merchandisers forced manufacturers into price deals that all but eliminated the profits at the manufacturer's level.

At the consumer level, the buyer of a Snapper lawn mower lost the benefit of the independent dealer who sold nothing but Snapper equipment and who offered repair and service facilities. The mass merchandisers provided no such service. If there were any problems with a lawn mower, Wal-Mart or Home Depot would tell the customers they should go elsewhere to have it repaired. The customer had no place to go and, of course, in many cases, he would never buy another Snapper lawn mower. Previously, every dealer was required to have service facilities, which are an important part of a consumer products company.

Scott also cut the cooperative advertising and marketing plan, which saved money in the short run but proved to be a foolish decision that only added to Snapper's financial woes over the long term. I do not know what the sales volume of Snapper is today, but I am certain it is only a fraction of what it was when I left Fuqua Industries in 1989. What happened to Snapper is the best illustration I know of how to destroy a company with a few stupid management decisions.

INTERSTATE MOTOR FREIGHT SYSTEMS

As the song says, "You need to know when to hold 'em, and know when to fold 'em." That advice is essential to business success. When we acquired Interstate Motor Freight Systems in 1968, it was a good deal and I went to extreme efforts to make it happen. But I also realized when it was time to get rid of the business.

The company, which was based in Grand Rapids, Michigan, operated a trucking line all over the country and in Canada. During one of my visits with John Archibald, my loan officer at Chase Manhattan Bank in New York, John mentioned that Interstate might be acquired because the bank's trust department controlled a large block of its stock.

I asked John if he would invite the trust officer in charge of the investment to meet us for a drink after work. We went across the street to a bar and as we talked I began to notice that John's associate liked to drink in a big way. I brought up the subject of Interstate Motor Freight Company, but the trust officer was cautious about even admitting that the bank owned 30 percent of the stock.

As we continued to talk, I knew that if I could get this man to go to dinner and keep drinking, I might have a chance at finding out more about Interstate Motor Freight Systems. Dinner was fine with him, so we went to Giambelli's on 50th Street and got the quietest table available. I began to urge more drinks on him while Archibald and I sipped ours. In due time, I brought up the matter of the Interstate Motor Freight stock and little by little I was able to get the associate to tell me how much stock the bank owned, how much he thought it was worth, and how we could buy it.

I waited a week and went back to New York to see John Archibald and the trust officer, and we worked out a deal to buy the bank's stock and make a tender for the remainder of the company. Perhaps I had used unusual methods to make the deal, but it was an excellent move for both Fuqua and the bank.

We acquired Interstate in 1968 when it had sales of about $50 million. In a few years we increased the revenues to more than $300 million. In this acquisition we used a combination of debentures, warrants, and common stock without any cash being involved.

I think I may have invented something new in the construction of the warrants. A warrant is like a stock option: it gives the right to buy stock at a certain price with an expiration date; it pays no dividends and has no voting rights. I constructed a warrant for Fuqua Industries that involved a unique feature: the company could reduce the amount of the exercise price temporarily or permanently. This meant that if

Fuqua Industries decided it needed the cash that might flow in from the exercise of the warrants, we could reduce the price per share at which the warrants could be used to buy a share of stock. In effect, this would force the conversion of the warrants into cash purchase of stock in the company. I saw this as a way to ensure that if things got tight and I needed the money, I could reduce the price below the market price of Fuqua stock and bring in cash. We never used this feature, but I think it was good insurance. I never knew of another company that had a warrant with that feature. For some reason, warrants have gone out of fashion and are seldom used anymore. At the same time, stock options have developed as an attractive incentive for management personnel. If a company distributed warrants among its stockholders, it would be the same as issuing stock options.

Interstate Motor Freight Systems remained profitable and it was unique among Fuqua companies by having its own financing arrangement with banks that would lend it up to 90 percent of the net fixed asset value of its trucks. Interstate was in a regulated industry, which meant the tariffs for carrying a particular commodity from one point to another were set by rating bureaus. Any company that was of average efficiency could make a reasonable profit.

In 1980, I was driving to the office when I heard on the radio that Senator Edward Kennedy was going to support a bill deregulating the trucking industry and I knew that if he backed it, it would probably pass. If that happened, I knew I wouldn't want to be in the trucking business. When I got to the office, I told my officers to immediately drop everything and prepare to spin out the trucking business to the stockholders so we wouldn't be in the business when deregulation became effective. If there were labor troubles from the Teamsters, the cost would get so high that the trucking companies would go broke. And indeed they did, but we had already gotten rid of Interstate and it didn't happen on my watch.

Other people in the business had the same information, but they did not act on it. They let the unions run the labor rates up to the point that trucking lines couldn't make any money. Those who are fortunate enough to make the right decisions are the ones who win the battle. I was in the unique position of being able to make decisions without having a committee debate them. I had never really had a boss since I was 21 years old, and I controlled large and small companies by dominating the situation. The conventional wisdom says you have to have 51 percent of a corporation to control it, but that's not true. In the various companies I controlled, I was not always the majority stockholder, but I made my own decisions. The boards of directors I had would be my friends and they didn't argue with anything I wanted to do. I made my own decisions, right and wrong, for my entire business career and never operated through committees. Sometimes I've been so good at foreseeing events that it's been sort of frightening. I guess it was a gift that I was born with.

THE TROJAN SEED COMPANY

The Trojan Seed Company is an excellent example of using

other people's money and taking advantage of the tax code in conducting business. We had always avoided high technology businesses at Fuqua Industries, but Trojan Seed became the exception. The company was headquartered in Olivia, Minnesota, and was operated by two young fellows who had put together a bunch of genetic engineers doing exciting things in developing hybrid seed corn. The process required scientific skills to mate different types of corn to produce the desired characteristics.

The acquisition of this company came about in 1969 as the result of a chance conversation one of our people had with Bob Roundhorst and Jake Jacobson, the two men who had started Trojan. At the time of acquisition, Trojan Seed had sales of $8 million and was growing at a fast pace. Roundhorst and Jacobson said they could grow at a rate of 25 percent per year for an indefinite period if they could get enough capital.

I made a contract with them to buy their company by giving them half of the value in stock then and by promising to give them just as many shares again at the end of five years if their performance justified it. All of this was done on a tax-free basis under the IRS rules. The Fuqua stock went up in the meantime and they made a lot of money out of it.

One thing we were interested in doing with Trojan Seed Company was producing a variety of corn that would grow in colder climates. In other words, we wanted to increase the growing season of corn. If one could imagine being able to plant corn, say, 100 miles farther north than was the current practice, the potential for increased productivity added up to a very large amount of corn.

We had our principal operation in Minnesota, but we also had a corn nursery in the Hawaiian Islands where corn could be planted every day of the year. We would plant the corn and, when it got to a certain height, it would be cross-pollinated with other corn that had different characteristics. This hybridization hopefully would produce an improved seed. We hired some very skilled scientists on a conditional basis in which they would receive bonuses for any improvements they developed in seed corn.

The strategy Trojan used to obtain rapid sales growth was very interesting. Trojan's management knew that the cost of the seed itself was a very small part of the total cost of a farmer growing a crop of corn. If the farmer could be convinced that the seed was even a little bit superior to his seed alternatives, he would be willing to pay a higher price because that extra amount would be insignificant to the cost of growing his crop. So Trojan always priced its seed higher than the competition in the belief that farmers would buy it on the basis that if the price was higher, it must be better.

Because Trojan also knew that farmers respected the opinions of the most successful farmers in their counties, the company succeeded in recruiting these farmers to be their farmer/dealers. As an extra incentive, Trojan initiated a program of premium giveaways, from a pocket knife for a dealer who sold one bag of seed to a trip for two to Hawaii for the farmer/dealer who sold 500 or more bags. The prospect of a trip to Hawaii from Minnesota in the dead of winter was plenty of incentive for the farmer/dealer to sell a lot of seed.

In another shrewd marketing move, Trojan had name-plates made for every corn farmer in Iowa and Minnesota. These nameplates came with a mounting bracket that would go on each farmer's mailbox. The accounts of the farmer/dealer were charged one dollar for each nameplate made for every farmer in that territory. The idea was that the dealer would go calling on each potential customer and give the nameplate away by suggesting they go down and mount it on the farmer's mail-box. Since the mailboxes were typically some distance from the house, the time it took to get to the mailbox and get the name-plate mounted was enough for the dealer to sell the farmer on the benefits of Trojan Seed.

We had fabulous success and were making out like bandits when along came the pharmaceutical companies wanting to get into the hybrid seed business. All the ones making animal pharmaceuticals decided they should be working with plant genetics also.

When we finally decided to sell Trojan, we met with some representatives from the Pfizer pharmaceutical company in New York to discuss the deal over dinner. Normally I would have expected the matter of price to come up early in the con-versation, but the Pfizer man spent all of his time telling me why they should be in the seed corn business. Finally, he said, "By the way, how much do you want for your seed company?" It surprised me, but I gave him a price considerably above what I would be willing to take. He said, "That's fine," and went on talking.

Pfizer subsequently proceeded to apply corporate practices to the seed corn company, eliminated performance bonuses, and ruined the entrepreneurial qualities that had made Trojan Seed a success. It is difficult for acquisitions to work well when the acquired company is run by real entrepreneurs and a big corporation attempts to change its operation into its multilayered management structure in an effort to get uniform results in different types of businesses.

The negotiation to sell Trojan Seed Company was a lesson in the importance of communication. Sometimes it pays to keep your mouth shut about the price until the motivated buyer brings it up — the potential buyer may be willing to pay a lot more than the seller really expects to get for the business.

CHAPTER 12

FUQUA INDUSTRIES AT THE TOP

CMEI AND PIER 1

The Conglomerate Era of 1965–1969 was followed by what might be characterized as the Real Estate Era of 1970–1974. Inflation in the U.S. had begun to accelerate in the late 1960s. The economy had been stimulated beyond its normal growth capacity by the combined high spending for social programs and the war in Vietnam.

As prices for property rose with inflation, real estate became a seemingly unbeatable investment. Using property as collateral, it was possible to borrow up to 100 percent of the purchase price to finance real estate purchases. The U.S. Congress helped to accelerate the attractiveness of real estate by permitting the creation of Real Estate Investment Trusts

(REITs). A REIT could invest directly in real estate or lend money for real estate development projects and avoid having to pay federal income taxes, so long as it paid at least 90 percent of its earnings to its shareholders.

Hundreds of REITs were established by banks and developers to avoid the double taxation on profits, and the REITs were leveraged to the hilt based on investments in and loans to what appeared to be a sure thing — real estate. But the Real Estate Era ended with the recession of 1974–1975. Property prices crashed and interest rates rose.

As real estate developments went into bankruptcy, they were taken over by their principal lenders — the REITs. Then, one after another, the REITs began to fold. Having given out 90 percent of their earnings to their shareholders and being highly leveraged themselves, they had virtually no reserves. Without profitable real estate projects, they had no real capacity to borrow. Only a handful of REITs survived the second half of the 1970s.

One of those who got caught in the REIT disaster was Tom Cousins, perhaps Atlanta's most successful developer. Cousins, who was on the board of Fuqua Industries, had a real estate investment trust called CMEI that was listed on the New York Stock Exchange. When the real estate crash hit, he had his name on the stock and everybody looked to him to do something. After running up a loss of more than $100 million, CMEI shareholders were facing financial disaster.

Cousins asked me if there was some way I could help him out and get the stock back to where it was. It was at $40 a share at one point and it had gotten down to less than $4. I told him Fuqua Industries would take on the management with an option to buy some percentage of CMEI at the then-market price, which would be fair to all the public stockholders. So we made a deal without our having to put up any money.

When I got into it, the money was all owed to the banks. At that time, banks couldn't get enough of those real estate loans and they had loaned money on property all over the country. I knew the banks didn't want us to go into bankruptcy, because that would cut them out, so I went from bank to bank with a proposal. I said, "Mr. Banker, here's a list of the properties we have. I'll give you this one and I'll give you that one in exchange for the loan. If you don't take it, I'm going to put the company into bankruptcy and you won't get anything." Every one of the banks accepted the deal, and I got rid of the $100 million debt.

The value to me was the tax loss that resulted. There was already a huge loss built up, and when we gave these buildings away, the loss on paper was enhanced. Anyway, we had a tax loss carry-forward that we could use to offset profits over a period of years. In other words, we wouldn't have to pay any income tax.

To maximize the benefits of this large tax loss carry-forward, I immediately began searching for a healthy, profitable business and ended up buying Pier 1 Import Stores. One of the first things I did was fly to Fort Worth to talk with Luther Henderson, who was the principal shareholder and CEO of Pier 1, and ask for a list of the profitability of the stores. There were about 250 stores in the chain, and only one third of them were profitable. I told Henderson to shut down the unprofitable ones, which he agreed to do, and then I asked him to see about making the interiors of the stores more attractive.

Henderson explained that the company was barely profitable because mass merchandisers such as K-mart and Wal-Mart had begun to import many of the same products that originally had been exclusive to Pier 1 Imports. I suggested that we upgrade the company's merchandise to bring about a greater sense of exclusivity for the shopper. In effect, we shut down the unprofitable stores, used the cash coming from these shutdowns to improve the appearance of the remaining stores, and began offering more products that would be less subject to competition from the K-marts and Wal-Marts.

Within a year, profits improved substantially and they were sheltered by the tax loss carry-forward of CMEI. The price of Pier 1's stock was rising, and Charles "Red" Scott called to ask if I was willing to sell Pier 1 to his company, Intermark, Inc. The stock in Pier 1 by that time had risen to a range of $5–$6 per share from our option price of $1.75. After a period of several months of negotiations, we sold Fuqua Industries' shares in Pier 1 for $12.25 per share to Intermark. Fuqua Industries made a profit of $35 million and we never put a penny of our own money into the whole deal.

CYPRUS CORPORATION

As I was developing Fuqua Industries, I was separately doing personal deals to expand my own growing net worth. One of the private business deals in which I was involved along the way was created when I bought control of two key companies on the American Stock Exchange that had nothing in them but cash. They had originally been set up to own stock in real estate investment trusts (REITs).

I kept my eyes open for situations like this. I felt that if I could get working control of an actively traded company, I could swap its stock for control of a business and increase the value substantially. I did this several times and part of my fortune was made in this manner.

My idea was that I would combine these companies and then sell a conventional corporate vehicle. These investment trusts were subject to a different set of rules by the SEC than regular corporations. The primary difference was that, with a closed-end investment trust, any significant change in the assets or the operation required approval by the SEC under a 1940 act of Congress. Regular corporations were treated differently: they only were required to make a full disclosure.

I changed the name of these two companies when they were consolidated to Cyprus Corporation. I can think of no reason why I chose the name Cyprus over some other, except that it put the listing at the bottom of the "Cs" in the newspaper stock tables. Although I was controller of many millions in cash, I had difficulty making acquisitions because I had to get approval from the SEC for every change we made. Eventually I decided it would not be practical to make a regular company out of the two real estate investment stock companies.

At the time I decided to sell Cyprus, I learned that Al

Rockwell, whom I had known in the Young Presidents Organization, had retired as head of the aerospace company Rockwell International and was looking for a vehicle to do just what I had planned to do. We reached an agreement wherein he paid me a significant amount for my control position in Cyprus. Rockwell put the cash to work in things related to the space program, but he never succeeded in developing this vehicle the way we both had thought was possible. Nevertheless, I made a nice sum for myself.

The Cyprus deal is included here because it was typical of the many business transactions I was involved in purely aside from Fuqua Industries. Fuqua Industries itself was not the principal source of my private fortune.

TRITON AND A GOOD SWAP

Triton Limited was one of the biggest real estate companies during the heyday of the REITs, and when it went under, it was the biggest real estate bankruptcy in history, about $1 billion. It had been sponsored by Chase Manhattan Bank, and when the company came out of bankruptcy it was renamed the Triton Group. The stockholders didn't get anything out of it. The bondholders who had the debentures got all of the stock in the new company. With a tax loss carry-forward of about $200 million, its only assets were a building in New Jersey that was leased to the government and a pretty piece of property on the southern end of Puerto Rico. The real estate property was what I ended up with after I bought enough bonds to control the company.

I didn't know a thing about the real estate business as far as what to do with it, but I did know what to do with a consumer products business. There was a fellow in Houston who was in the real estate development business and who owned the Simplicity Pattern Co. I cold-called him and said, "Look, you're in the real estate development business and I know about consumer products. Why don't we talk about swapping your consumer products business for my real estate business?" I convinced him that if he took the company, he would have as much as $100 million in a tax loss to use for his development business. It wasn't a simple transaction, but we swapped and the deal turned out to be good for both of us.

NATIONAL INDUSTRIES

Many of the conglomerates stumbled during the recessions of the early 1970s and Wall Street's fascination with these types of companies began to fade. One of the problems was that entrepreneurs who were good at making acquisitions were not necessarily good at running companies. Some entrepreneurs who were successful on their own did not like being part of a corporate structure. Securities professionals who watched the rapidly rising earnings per share of the conglomerates in the late 1960s were not happy when those earnings could not be sustained during recessions or in a period of declining acquisition activity.

Fuqua Industries went through a slimming-down phase in the mid-1970s in which we got rid of many of our unprofitable subsidiaries. Then we began looking for an acquisition target that would be a conglomerate, much as Fuqua Industries had been in 1975, with a broad base of operations. If we could acquire such a company, we knew we could create value by selling off the bad companies and keeping the good ones.

In 1977 I found the perfect company. National Industries, which was headquartered in Louisville, Kentucky, had several subsidiaries that I thought would be of interest to us. I had seen an item in the *Wall Street Journal* saying the CEO had recently died. National had been having some earnings problems, but my informal study of the company caused me to believe I could do something with it. With the death of the CEO, there appeared to be no one to contact to see if we could make some kind of deal. However, in the proxies filed with the SEC, one director's name had been listed for the past 15 years, while all the other directors had been listed only for a few years. It seemed reasonable that the longest tenured director would be the person to approach.

His name was Barney Barnett, a Louisville attorney, and I cold-called him and said I would like to negotiate to acquire National Industries. He obviously was interested, so Carl Sanders and I flew to Louisville to discuss the deal. Our timing turned out to be perfect. Barnett told us they had promoted one of the National officers to CEO, but he had terminal cancer. We decided that the temporary CEO, Joe Gammon, should be brought into our negotiations, but otherwise we four would be the only ones involved.

We agreed that Fuqua Industries would acquire National in a merger wherein National stockholders would get one-half the purchase price in cash and one-half in Fuqua common stock. So careful were we to keep the deal just between the four of us that when I called a board meeting on a Sunday afternoon and National did the same, no other directors of either Fuqua or National knew what the meeting was for. In this way, we were able to make the deal quietly without any competition, which is what Barnett and Gammon wanted as badly as we did.

LARRY KLAMON

"This was a typical J. B. deal in the sense that there was one person who was the chairman of the board that J. B. could sit down with and negotiate. He would not do well in the current environment of auctions and so forth. J.B's style was to sit down with the decision maker and to take his measure and to try to do a transaction. He'd come back with all these scribblings on a yellow legal pad and say, 'Here's the deal.' It was our job to go out and get it done."

We acquired this company with $1 billion in sales for $67 million, or $40 million below its book value of $107 million. National's subsidiaries included such things as the Cott beverage corporation, a chain of retail stores, and a gasoline brokerage business. Now, Fuqua had a liquidation to do, but because the National businesses we wanted to sell were so visible and we were in a period of easy financing, buyers lined up in a hurry. Within a year we had recovered all of the cash we had put into the deal, and we still owned the most valuable assets.

LANO AND THE STRANGE MR. ALKEK

One of the most interesting and profitable subsidiaries of National Industries was Lano, a petroleum distributor that bought and traded large inventories of gas and stored them in tanks and pipelines. It would buy a million gallons of gasoline from a Gulf refinery on a Friday afternoon and on Monday it would resell part or all of the gasoline to Texaco or some other company for a few pennies per gallon more than it paid Gulf for its excess inventory. Or, in some cases, it would sell the Gulf excess inventory to an independent gasoline distributor, such as the 7-11 stores. The value of the business was essentially the value of the inventory at any given time.

The manager of Lano was Albert Alkek, who lived in a tiny suite in a Houston hotel during the week and commuted to his ranch on weekends. Alkek had an office in a small building in Houston, but there was no identification of Lano on the building, nor was Alkek's name listed anywhere.

Alkek was a shrewd trader who had made a huge fortune buying and selling the stock of the major oil companies. We worked out a compensation deal whereby Alkek would continue to run the business with no salary, but would receive 25 percent of the pretax profits.

Lano had a small operations and accounting office in a little town a considerable distance from Houston while Alkek and two female employees ran the Houston office. What I had to go through to get to see Alkek and this risky business I had bought is a story in itself. Because there was no sign, I had to count the doors from the stairway to the outer entrance of his office. This door had two locks requiring two different keys, and there was a second door inside identical to the outer door, separated by a dummy hallway. Once inside, one of the women acted as a sort of guard who let visitors into Alkek's office through yet another locked door. Another door in Alkek's very modest office opened into a huge walk-in vault. On one of my visits when we were negotiating the deal, he took me into the vault to show me that he was as rich as he claimed to be.

It was an incredible sight. There were stacks of stock certificates from floor to ceiling, representing millions of dollars in value. I think many of the certificates were from the Sinclair Oil Co. that Alkek had gotten when he sold Sinclair Oil and gas properties years before. He trusted nobody, and thus he had kept all of these old-fashioned stock certificates where he could see and touch them. I have known many rich men, but he is the only one I ever knew who showed me such overwhelming evidence of raw cash wealth. Needless to say, I was convinced.

Lano was really a high-risk business, but I had evaluated the risks and determined they were more than offset by the potential profits. During 1979, oil prices doubled and Lano did $1 billion in sales and had a pretax profit of $120 million, even with the almost minute margins inherent in the broker-age business. In that year alone, we paid Alkek $30 million in compensation according to the contract we had made.

Despite these great profits, the oil distribution business was so nerve-wracking that after a time I determined I would have to get out of it. I decided to discuss the matter with Alkek one weekend when he had invited Dottie and me to stay with him and his wife Margaret at his ranch. That Saturday afternoon, we drove to the top of a little mountain on his place where he had a one-room shack stocked with whiskey and playing cards. Fortunately, there were also some pads of legal paper that I used to make a major contract that very afternoon.

We stopped in and relaxed over a couple of drinks. Then I told Albert I wanted him to buy his company back (he had originally sold it to National Industries). I wrote on a legal pad that he was to buy back the business for $180 million in cash, but only after I agreed to throw in a jet plane did he agree to the deal. It amounted to a few million dollars, but the sale of Lano not only would be profitable to Fuqua Industries, it would certainly add years to my life. I brought the penciled, legal-pad copy of the agreement back to Atlanta, and on Monday morning I turned it over to our general counsel and told him and the other Fuqua officers to take care of the details.

That Saturday night, however, before Dottie and I returned to Atlanta, Albert and I decided to celebrate the closing of the deal with a couple of drinks. He had a locked bar at his ranch home that he unlocked to make the drinks, and then promptly locked again. When we decided it was time for a second drink, he went through the same process of opening and locking the bar. You would think a man with as much money as he had would not go to all that trouble, but that was simply one of his eccentricities.

Alkek was always listed in the Forbes 400 and he gave away vast amounts to charities while he was alive and left substantial sums in his will when he died. But he was also a high roller. When Dottie and I went with Margaret and him to Las Vegas on two occasions, he did not register at the hotel under his real name, but he obviously was well known to the staff, who put us in the fanciest suite I have ever stayed in. Alkek made only $10,000 bets and he won or lost several hundred thousand dollars in an evening. Dottie and I traveled with Albert and Margaret to a casino in London once when he won $250,000 in one night, and cleaned out all the American currency the casino had. I later confirmed this in a conversation with the casino's manager. I have met many interesting characters during my years in business, but Albert Alkek was one of the most unusual.

GEORGIA FEDERAL

I first became interested in buying Georgia Federal in 1984 when the bank announced it would go public. I had wanted to own a bank ever since my experience with Willingham Finance Co. in Augusta when I was forced to kowtow to big financial institutions for loans, and Georgia Federal looked like an ideal investment.

I obtained a copy of the prospectus as soon as I could and began going over the figures for earnings, growth, and losses for a certain period of years. Georgia Federal was the largest S&L in the state and it had always made profits until 1982. It had huge losses in 1982 and 1983, which seemed strange in light of the fact that Georgia Federal otherwise had an uninterrupted stream of earnings. I felt that there must be more to the story, so I went up Peachtree Street in Atlanta to the Federal Home Loan Bank, which was the supervisory institution for the whole Southeast, and looked at the more detailed filings of Georgia Federal. I saw right away that the losses were strictly an aberration and were not a result of bad loans. Georgia Federal's losses in 1982 and 1983 were primarily from hedging activities of the bank that turned out to be very unprofitable. However, these figures were not broken out in the ordinary financial statement shown in their prospectus.

It was not possible under the then-existing regulations for an individual to own more than 10 percent of a federal savings and loan. Georgia Federal stock, which was coming on the market, seemed like a great investment opportunity. At the same time, I convinced Dave Thomas, my friend and neighbor from Fort Lauderdale and the founder of Wendy's Hamburgers chain, to buy 5 percent of the stock. After the initial offering, the price went up to reflect the current good earnings of Georgia Federal. Our combined 15 percent made us very important to Georgia Federal and, when the stock came to market, I asked to be put on the board of directors.

The company prospered, and in two years the price of Georgia Federal stock had increased significantly. I decided that it was such a large profit-producer that it should be owned by Fuqua Industries rather than by me personally. Georgia Federal stock had been trading for around $13 or $14 per share, but we made an initial offer of $18 and, after some negotiation, we settled on a price of $21 per share. Fuqua Industries acquired all of the Georgia Federal stock for $175 million in cash and operated the company as a subsidiary. I personally made $16 million on the deal and Dave Thomas made $8 million.

The Georgia Federal deal is an example of the importance of looking beyond raw figures. In fact, the first thing I look at in a financial statement is the auditor's footnotes because that is where any irregularities are presented. If I had not gone to the Federal Home Loan Bank, I would never have known that the losses Georgia Federal had shown in its regular statement came from something besides its regular operations, and I would not have bought into the company. That is how money is made.

One of the next things I did was to convince the board of Georgia Federal to acquire First Family Finance Company as a subsidiary. First Family, which was very profitable, handled consumer business, such as installment sales contracts from furniture and appliance retailers. There are several reasons that individuals would prefer to borrow from a consumer finance business like First Family rather than a regular bank. First of all, these customers are usually blue-collar, working-class people who feel uncomfortable walking into marble lobbies of big banks where everyone is wearing a suit. Second, many people do not like discussing their financial situation with a young college graduate who they may feel is looking down his nose at them. And, finally, most bankers are not interested in offering loans for less than $1,500, so they tell their customers to put that amount on their Visa or MasterCard. Well, the customers who go to First Finance may not have credit cards.

While business was good at Georgia Federal in the mid-'80s, the situation for S&Ls in general was getting worse. Every day it seemed there was another story in the newspapers about a failing S&L and how much it was going to cost the taxpayers to bail out these institutions. We did not think the stigma of the S&Ls would help the price of Fuqua Industries stock so, in 1988, we decided to sell Georgia Federal. After some months, we sold it to First Financial Management for $225 million, which was a nice profit, after having made $50 million a year from Georgia Federal for Fuqua Industries. Georgia Federal later became a part of what was the Citizens & Southern National Bank as the consolidation of the banking industry took place. One mistake we made was in not selling off the First Family consumer finance company before we sold Georgia Federal. First Financial Management sold that company later and recaptured a large portion of the cost of buying Georgia Federal. Of course, Fuqua Industries got no benefit from that transaction.

However, not only was the Georgia Federal deal

extremely profitable to Fuqua Industries and to me personally, but it also resulted in a windfall for The Fuqua School of
Business at Duke University. Shortly after I had sold my
stock in Georgia Federal, I decided that Dave Thomas would
be a good prospect for the endowment Duke needed to get a
conference center for the business school. I arranged to have
dinner with Dave at his home in Columbus, Ohio, and after
the meal I went into his den and made my pitch. I told him
that since he had made $8 million in the Georgia Federal
deal, I wanted half of that profit to be given to Duke
University for the R. David Thomas Conference Center.
Before I left, I had a commitment from him for $4 million
and now Duke University's business school has one of the
finest conference centers in the country.

RECREATIONAL PRODUCTS

In the early years of Fuqua Industries, we got into recreational
products because I felt that, with the growing amount of
leisure time American workers were getting in this period of
economic prosperity, the market for products and services
used for recreation would be booming. In addition to owning
Martin Theaters, we developed our business into a major share
of boats, from the smallest vessels to 65-foot yachts. We also
entered into a joint venture with a Japanese steel company to
manufacture yachts and other types of pleasure boats for the
Pacemaker Yacht Co., which we had bought from the Leek
family in Egg Harbour, New Jersey.

We assumed — wrongly, it turned out — that if we gave

the steel company the blueprints and plans for the boats, they would be able to go ahead without any supervision on our part. Some months into the project, we sent somebody from the Pacemaker factory to Japan to see how they were coming along with their manufacturing efforts.

Among other things, our man saw a boat suspended from a crane 70 or 80 feet in the air. He asked our Japanese counterpart what the purpose of that was and the man gleefully told him they were testing boats. It seems the Japanese had seen copies of some ads we had run showing a boat being released from a helicopter into the ocean and they thought this was how we tested the construction of the boats. They did not realize it was just an attention-getter in a magazine ad. Despite this somewhat humorous misunderstanding, we found the Japanese to be good partners.

Eventually Fuqua Industries expanded into companies that made team sporting goods for almost every sport. These products included everything from golf and exercise equipment, bicycles, and baseball and football gear to other recreational products such as pool tables and bowling balls. In 1979, Fuqua Industries had about 25 subsidiaries and we had a good operation in China where we made things that required a lot of labor, such as backpacks, tents, boots, rainwear, and other labor-intensive products. We also had a company that made springs for recreational vehicles and processed steel for industrial use.

All of the import operations were under the supervision of Melvin Marx, who was president of Fuqua World Trade Corp. We had offices in most of the Far East countries, including Japan, China, Taiwan, and Korea. I visited every one of these offices at some time myself so that the people in the field would know of my genuine interest in what they did. There's also another reason that I showed up at plants and distribution centers for the various manufacturing operations that we had: I have always believed in the saying that a farmer's footprints are the best fertilizer.

All of these acquisitions were financed by the use of preferred stock, subordinated debentures, warrants, and common stock, and of course plain old cash. We had such a good credit reputation that we had banks practically running over each other trying to get a piece of our business. We did do considerable business with a Japanese bank that we found to be very cooperative.

We also had a line of credit with several European banks. Our ratio of debt to equity (stock and subordinated debt) varied from time to time, depending on which acquisitions we were making. But we never had any difficulty raising money for any acquisitions we proposed to make.

One of the risk factors in recreational products is that it is a fashion business. What sells well today may not find much of a market five years from now. This means that our sporting goods companies were continually developing new products to hold and gain market share. Even the types of sports that are popular change, and a business is subject to the risk of obsolescence unless management is willing to develop new products to keep up with current trends.

DOING BUSINESS ABROAD

I had always tried to create a family feeling among the presidents and key people in Fuqua Industries by making our annual business meetings pleasant social occasions as well. We usually held these meetings in some nice location, such as Sea Island, Georgia, but in the 1980s, I decided the board needed to go to Russia and China to see for themselves the difference between capitalism and communism. Dottie and I had been to Russia in the 1970s, and the trip had been a real eye-opener. I felt that we might be doing business with Russia at some point since we were already manufacturing some sporting goods products in China.

We held the Russian meeting at the American Embassy in Moscow in 1985, and I arranged for our board to get a real flavor of the economic and social system of the country. In 1983, I had taken the board to China. I lined up a number of activities to give the board members and their wives a real thrill. We did some sightseeing and hosted a dinner for the Chinese we did business with — but of course they had to have a dinner to reciprocate. Until you have been to a real Chinese banquet, you cannot imagine how hospitable the people can be.

LARRY KLAMON

"The trip to China was an interesting one and it helped create great esprit de corps. We were one of the early companies to have an office in China. We established a buying office in Beijing in 1979, and the staff were young Americans who spoke Mandarin. They didn't know much about sporting goods, but their job was to help us locate suppliers and help us deal with the bureacracy. The first time I went to Beijing in 1979, you could hardly get a taxi. The last time I was there a few years later, you'd arrive at the airport and there would be a fleet of silver Toyotas. We were never a huge international company, but the sporting goods business was significant because it allowed us to be competitive."

I got into China at the most appropriate time. As soon as President Carter normalized commercial relations with China in 1979, I was almost on the next plane to see what I could set up in the way of some business operation. I viewed that country as a source of cheap labor and, at some point, as a huge market for our products.

I took Melvin Marx, president of our sporting goods subsidiary, and an interpreter and, although I knew no one there, I had no difficulty finding my way around the Chinese system. On this first trip I stayed at the Peking Hotel — it was Peking then, Beijing now — and I set up a meeting with several Chinese leaders. I also lined up a nice office with a teletype and telephone, which was fortunate because few offices were available. We were one of only 10 American companies to obtain such facilities. Those who waited until after the embargo was lifted had to confine themselves to a room at the Peking Hotel and the use of a common teletype.

I had two young men with me who would become our initial employees in China, and we met with these Chinese leaders for several days. In addition to English and Chinese, my associates spoke French, which was handy because we knew that some of the Chinese, if not all, would understand the English conversation between myself and the interpreters. Having the two young men speak French enabled them to consult among themselves and decide how they would interpret something the Chinese had said.

Our entry into China is a good example of the value of being willing and able to move once you see an opportunity. We had profitable and pleasant dealings with the Chinese for years, and the cost of labor in China was so low that we were able to produce sporting goods much more profitably than we would have if we had had them manufactured in the U.S.

Doing business in other countries was always interesting, especially when we began dealing with the Mexicans. We had acquired a Georgia company called Rome Enterprises that made attachments and equipment for Caterpillar tractors, and we opened a plant in Mexico City. As part of the cost of doing business, we had to put the equivalent of the local IRS agent on our payroll and, in order to import anything from the U.S. into Mexico, we had to pay not only tariffs but a bonus to the Customs people.

CHAPTER 13

THE FALL OF FUQUA INDUSTRIES

AN ATTEMPTED COUP

At the beginning of the '80s, it was clear to me that conglomerates were no longer popular, that most of the growth in the value of Fuqua Industries (FQA) stock was past, and that in the future we could grow the earnings and yet not see the price of the stock change very much. The answer to this was to de-conglomerate.

My thought was that I would retire from the company at some point and let Larry Klamon, whom I had made chairman and chief executive officer, run the company with a simple financial structure and no debt. This would give him a good business with the resources with which to develop another company.

LARRY KLAMON

"One of J. B.'s unique strengths is that as the world has changed, he has changed with it. He was a conglomerator, and he built a conglomerate. But he was also willing to be the leader of the band in shrinking it. He has been successful because he was willing to go where the facts led him."

As I sold subsidiaries, Fuqua Industries was accumulating a nice cash kitty. Because the stock market was going through a recession in the early '80s, I decided that the best way to use this cash was to buy Fuqua Industries stock. At a meeting with the board of directors, I outlined a plan for a major buyback of our stock. It soon became clear that the discussion had gotten confused as a "going private" proposal by me. Several FQA senior officers viewed this as an opportunity to do a leveraged buyout themselves, leaving me personally outside with no interest.

On Friday, July 31, 1981, I had all trading in Fuqua Industries stock suspended in what turned out to be one of the most troubling episodes in my business career. Three of our officers, President Kay Slayden, General Counsel Rod Dowling, and Treasurer Dave Fraser, had gone to the buyout firm Fortsmann-Little and gotten them to make an offer to buy all of the FQA shares in a leveraged buyout. Fortsmann-Little showed up at the board meeting with this outlandish proposal — subject to financing — and other ridiculous, unacceptable terms. The three officers would be fronting for the new owner, but I was to be left out entirely.

Apparently Slayden and the other two officers had sold Fortsmann on the idea that the board meeting would vote to eliminate me from my own company. The board was as amazed as I was at the whole idea and rejected the entire thing. The result of this palace rebellion was that Dowling and Fraser resigned; Sladen was terminated.

The publicity could not have been worse. Headlines in the newspapers read "Fuqua Rejects $25 Per Share Bid in Favor of His Own $20 Per Share Proposal for a Leveraged Buyout." The public perception was that the officers had been fired because they disagreed with me. The truth was, the board had rejected the Forstmann-Little offer because it was contingent on too many variables. There was no assurance that the financing could be lined up to support a $25 price and, in fact, it was the judgment of the board that it was highly unlikely that financing could be arranged at such a high price. Second, Forstmann-Little had accomplished only two relatively small $10 million transactions and did not have a track record that would give them credibility. There are more details to the story, but in summary I was challenged by some of my own officers and the rebels lost big.

This event brought on one of the worst episodes of depression I had ever experienced, but I proceeded with my plans that included raising enough cash by selling an asset to be able to buy in a major amount of the FQA shares via a self-tender offer at $20 per share. This was well above the $14–$15 FQA had been selling for. My belief in using other people's money was again going into action. If I had done a leveraged buyout, which I never seriously thought of doing, I would have had a major part of my net worth tied up in FQA when this was the obvious (to me) way of not only increasing my ownership of FQA shares, but doing it at no cost to myself.

The first thing I did was to sell Lano Corporation, a major subsidiary, for $180 million cash. Next, FQA offered to buy about 25 percent of its own shares at $20 per share, one-third more than it was trading for on the NYSE. It was a fine price for any stockholder who wanted to take a good profit. But the self-tender offer provided that FQA had the right to accept any or all of the shares tendered at the same price. This meant that all FQA stockholders could sell all of their shares and every stockholder was being treated alike and no pro-ration.

LARRY KLAMON

"The stock was trading around 13, and we had this big amount of cash. If we didn't do something, people who had bought the stock in anticipation of a $20 price would get rid of it and the price would go a lot lower. So we bought back 9 million of the 13 million outstanding shares. It used up most of our cash and our equity shrank from $262 million to $60 million, but what that did was to shrink the number of shares dramatically."

About 70 percent of all FQA shares were bought and cancelled. This meant that all FQA earnings would be divided among far fewer shares. FQA's per-share earnings skyrocketed and the stock began to trade at a much higher price than its pre-tender price! My own additional investment was zero. I would have been a fool to do a leveraged buyout or let the palace guard take the company away from me.

RED SCOTT AND THE END OF FUQUA INDUSTRIES

In 1988, I was 70 years old and had been thinking that a successful man my age should get out of his company and turn the management over to someone else. I had been selling off subsidiaries for several years and had slimmed down Fuqua Industries to the point where it was much smaller than it had been, but all units were making a good profit.

I had determined that a man named Charles "Red" Scott would be a good prospect to buy my interest in Fuqua Industries. He was indeed always after me to sell to him. He had two public companies that, on the surface, seemed to have done phenomenally well. They had adequate cash and other assets to buy me out, but I did not know at the time that in fact the companies were disasters. My greatest concern was that I not sell the company to anyone who would not take care of the management staff I had assembled and would not continue the good reputation of Fuqua Industries. I talked myself into believing that Scott, who was an entrepreneur like myself, fit this requirement.

We made a deal for substantially all of my shares in

Fuqua Industries at a price that was about the maximum the stock had ever sold for. In retrospect, I will forever wish that I had sold the whole company instead of falling into a bear trap with Red Scott. I could have delivered control and should have asked for a higher premium.

LARRY KLAMON

"After Red approached J. B. about buying his interest, they finally agreed on a price of $38 a share. The stock was trading in the high 20s, and it looked like a situation where J. B. got a very good deal and here was somebody who was going to leave the management intact. What we learned in hindsight was that Red's company, Intermark, had bought a couple of businesses that were absolute disasters and it was in serious trouble. They had bought a chain of steakhouses for $95 million and it turned out to be worth practically zilch. And they had bought a big liquor retailer in California out of bankruptcy and that was another disaster. Intermark went through more than $100 million and they ultimately were going to go into bankruptcy."

Of course, we didn't know about any of this at the time. Everything was going along smoothly after I agreed to sell, but I was getting increasingly nervous as I looked at Scott's other business transactions. He was the kind of person who could sell refrigerators to Eskimos, and he talked a good game to our corporate officers. After a few months, however, they began to see Scott in a different light. Larry Klamon had been made chief executive officer with the approval of Red Scott and the understanding that the company would continue to operate in the manner that it had for the past 25 years. I also had an understanding with Scott that if Klamon did not perform as CEO in the manner that Scott wanted, I would go along with removing him from that position. Larry had understood that to be the case also.

Scott did not propose to make changes in a way that would continue good morale in the company. He decided he would take over the management himself, even though he had no experience in actually operating a company.

We had a meeting of the board scheduled for Wednesday, February 6, 1991, in Orlando, where the Qualex subsidiary was having its annual management meeting. It was supposed to be a routine board meeting. The Sanders, the Klamons, and Dottie and I flew from Atlanta to Orlando and arrived at the meeting place shortly before 4 P.M. We had all been together from the time we left Atlanta until we got to the Fuqua board meeting in Orlando. Neither Sanders nor Klamon told me what they knew would take place at the board meeting. The only things on the agenda were routine housekeeping matters. When the meeting opened, Red Scott was presently chairman of the board and Larry Klamon was president and CEO. Scott had his three directors, including himself, Clark Johnson, and Tom Warner. The other three directors were myself, Carl Sanders, and Larry Klamon.

Red Scott began by announcing that he and Larry Klamon would be exchanging positions. This was just an unbelievable development, and it stunned Larry and me. I immediately saw that something had been going on behind my back, but I assumed that nothing significant could take place because the directors' votes should fall along party lines: Scott's three for the proposal and my three against it. Amazingly, when the vote was taken, it was 4 to 2. I produced only two votes, because one of my directors voted with Scott. This action meant that I was effectively thrown out of my own company — not because Scott would become CEO, but because I would not have at least three votes on my side. The intent, and indeed the effect, of this one board resolution was that my career at Fuqua Industries was terminated. In fact, within a month I was gone from Fuqua Industries — forever.

Scott also told Colin Brown that he was fired as general counsel. We had been expecting this, however, because Scott did not like a legal opinion that Brown had given at a previous board meeting. The only unusual thing that I later learned in connection with these events was that Scott and a number of his associates, along with one of my directors, had been seen in a restaurant in Atlanta the previous night. The dinner meeting included a lady lawyer from the Sanders firm who de facto became the general counsel of Fuqua Industries.

On the following morning back in Atlanta, a group of Scott's associates showed up at the Fuqua Industries headquarters in the Georgia Pacific Building and demanded such things as keys, credit cards, and other items that would be involved in a takeover of a small business. Scott announced to the Atlanta newspapers that he was taking over the company and that he would make many changes. He added that he was "going in with a blowtorch" to clean out people. The employees at the corporate headquarters of Fuqua Industries had no alternative but to go along with Scott. My own career of having built a multibillion-dollar conglomerate from a $12 million brick and tile manufacturer was clearly ending.

It all came to a head at a board meeting in Atlanta a week later when I initiated the termination clause in my contract and got out of the company altogether. Within a few months, Scott had completely destroyed the Fuqua Industries organization. He fired all the senior people and much of the entire staff on the theory that there was waste under Larry Klamon's and my operation.

LARRY KLAMON

"It was a surprise to J. B. and myself and a great disappointment to the corporate staff. J. B. left the board in March, I left 60 days later, and most of the corporate staff either left or were asked to leave. In the ensuing three years, Red Scott managed to lose hundreds of millions, and the company was on its way to bankruptcy when his own hand-picked board booted him out."

When I left Fuqua Industries, all subsidiaries were operating profitably and the company had nearly $400 million in cash and a contracted credit line of $200 million. Scott's first big mistake, which I discussed earlier, was changing the management at Snapper and instituting a policy that cut out the distributors and sold equipment directly to mass merchandisers such as Wal-Mart and Home Depot.

In a matter of two years, Fuqua Industries was well on the skids. Scott used up all of the cash, he lost the credit line contract, and he alienated Kodak, which was Fuqua's partner in Qualex, the photofinishing business. Meanwhile, Scott was having troubles with his two other companies and they were also on the way to bankruptcy. In order to raise cash, Scott got his handpicked board of directors at Fuqua Industries to lend him $40 million secured by Fuqua stock. Of course, this was contrary to all legal standards of insider trading and the company never recovered the $40 million.

From the time I was 21 years old, I had been the master of my own destiny in business. I had accomplished this by proving to my employees, shareholders, and corporate directors that my commitment and leadership created superior financial opportunities and rewards for my companies' shareholders. The way my ouster was orchestrated was hurtful to me personally but, more important, the career consequences to so many dedicated company employees and the eventual losses experienced by my shareholders were devastating. Many of Fuqua Industries' shareholders had invested in me and my team for many years and they had been handsomely rewarded. I had always felt proud that the name "Fuqua" was identified with success. Even though I was pushed out, my name and my pride were at risk. Seeing what I had created with such hard work destroyed by this new group was the most disappointing and depressing experience of my entire business career.

When Fuqua Industries had run out of working capital and was facing bankruptcy, along came Jack Phillips, who put several million dollars of his own money into the company and took it over to try to save it from bankruptcy. It was not a simple task. The only thing that Fuqua Industries had at that point that could produce substantial money was its half-interest in Qualex, which it owned with Kodak.

Red Scott could never have made a deal with Kodak and, had they done nothing, Kodak would have fallen into owner-ship of all of Qualex. This was a business with sales of about $700 million and was by far the most valuable property Fuqua Industries had. Phillips came to me and asked me if I would help him sell Fuqua's 50 percent share to Kodak. I took Phillips in my airplane to Rochester, New York, where we met with the chairman of Kodak and worked out a deal that brought Fuqua Industries about $300 million in cash. That saved the day for the immediate future.

Watching a company I had built up over more than two decades be destroyed in such a manner was devastating to me and took years off my life. I have earlier admitted that I have lots of ego, and I make no apology for that. If I don't think well of myself, I have no right to expect others to do so. Red Scott was well on his way to wrecking Fuqua Industries. In fact, it was clear to me — and I knew the company extremely well — that Fuqua Industries would run out of cash and would have to put itself into bankruptcy. I did not want my name connected with such a situation, so I offered Scott $1 million to sell me the name Fuqua Industries, Inc. Initially he refused this proposal and made fun of it. Time took care of that also. It was not too many months later that Scott had Carl Sanders call me and tell me he was willing to change the company name in exchange for $1 million in cash. My name might not be worth much to others, but it was worth $1 million to me. And that is how I bought back my name and Fuqua Industries was renamed the Actava Company. Phillips later made a deal with the businessman John Kluge to merge Actava into Kluge's company, Metromedia International. Fuqua Industries continued to deteriorate and no longer exists. The only thing left is the Snapper lawn mower business, which has been for sale for 10 years.

CHAPTER 14

OTHER SUCCESSES AND MISTAKES ALONG THE WAY

FATHER-AND-SON DEALS

It is important for people who are confident of accumulating a few million dollars to begin early to transfer a reasonable part of their assets to their children. I did this for my children when they were in their early teens. Because of the way I have run my affairs, my son Rex is a multimillionaire and an astute business-man in his own right.

The biggest transfer to my son was my deal to sell the Augusta cable TV system to him for $5 million in 1980 when I sold WJBF. He subsequently sold the cable system in 1985 for about $60 million cash. I had bought the franchise in 1965 because I knew that cable television was destined to become a very profitable business.

The cable system increased in value rapidly as subscribers were added, but the cost of construction required large outlays of cash. Cash was readily available from the television operation, so I did not personally have to put up any money. I had wanted to transfer some of my growing wealth to my son. Rex was already a millionaire several times over when a great opportunity came along and I decided to sell him the cable television system.

When Rex got out of the University of Georgia at the age of 21, I asked him to go to what was then known as the Fulton National Bank in Atlanta and borrow $1 million on his signature. I told him that if they asked him what he was going to do with it, he should tell them he was going into some deals with me, and that he did not have any specific thing in mind.

REX FUQUA

"I didn't know any better than not to go to the bank. I figured all they could do was tell me 'No.' The lesson that was drummed into my head from the time I was little was to be a leader, never be a follower. The other thing was the importance of dealing with people person to person. My father was never shy from the beginning about making an appointment and going to see somebody."

I was surprised when he came back from the bank with a commitment of $1 million, but he had accumulated substantial means because I had been giving him opportunities to make money since before he was college age. For example, in the late 1960s and early 1970s, I developed an independent oil and gas production operation. In simple terms, I was drilling oil and gas wells. I would buy a lease on a tract of land and drill a test well. If it looked like it would be a productive site, I would have an agreement drawn up so that Rex got all the profits. When we bought a lease and test wells indicated it would not be profitable, I took the losses. This is how we structured the partnership agreement between us.

REX FUQUA

"We were partners, theoretically, because when I got involved in the business, I told him I wouldn't work for him. Actually, I didn't plan on going into business until after my brother was killed and it was pretty clear there was no one else to go into the business but me. I had planned on going to law school, but my father shamed me into changing my mind by saying, 'Son, you don't become a lawyer. You hire a lawyer.' So that was the end of that."

We drilled wells in Texas, Louisiana, Arkansas, and other areas that were productive for gas and oil. I financed this operation by getting engineering reports that indicated what the anticipated value might be on a property that we intended to lease. I had investors to whom I would sell shares in oil and gas leases for anywhere from $5,000 and up.

I structured the agreement so that these investors got the depreciation from the cost of drilling. Even if we drilled a dry hole, they would have those "intangibles" — the cost of drilling the hole — to write off against their personal income. This is historically how even the major oil companies financed their drilling. There were good profits as well as tax benefits involved in such partnerships. I changed all of my interests in this business to a publicly traded company and got out of the business when banks were lending money on the basis of $100-a-barrel projected selling price of oil. I knew enough about the business and the engineering to know that, while we may have some periods when oil and gas were selling at high prices, there would be periods when they would sell at low prices — and there was no justification for the $100-a-barrel prediction.

Rex had had a part in these operations. We had a simple system whereby Rex got a preferred position in various investments I made, so that by the time he was out of college he had accumulated a nice sum of money. The loan of $1 million I told him to get was not unusual, except that I had anticipated the bank would require collateral. It made me feel good that my name could be used as capital by my son. In this way I was able to transfer capital to Rex.

Over a period of years, we transferred a little amount day by day from my estate to his by my doing such things as picking up the dinner check and paying for small items. All of this adds up and will increase the wealth of your children while not affecting the standard of living for you and your spouse.

There are so many ways in which a fertile mind can figure out how to transfer money from one generation to another. For example, if I saw a good speculative real estate deal, instead of putting it in my name I might put it in Rex's name and lend him the equity he needed to buy it. One of the ways that fortunes have been made is by buying real estate on an interest-only basis. It is worth paying an extra amount if it looks like a good deal.

There are a number of ways to honestly transfer money from one generation to another within the tax laws. For instance, grandparents can pay for all of the schooling and for such things as piano lessons for a grandchild. This is in addition to individuals being able to make annual gifts of $10,000 — or $20,000 by couples — to grandchildren, or literally anyone for any purpose. Even businessmen of modest means can give these sums to their grandchildren or nephews and nieces or other loved ones, whether they are family members or not.

Also, money can be transferred to children by means of loans. At one point, I made a very large loan to my son Rex, who earned a great return on it and paid me back. It cost me nothing, but it accomplished a goal that, so long as there are inheritance taxes, we all need to have.

THE ENERGY BUSINESS

In 1970, Rex and I decided that there were big profits to be made in the escalating value of energy companies. We had already been drilling oil and gas wells on our own, but we needed more capital. We set up a new corporation that we called HyTech Energy Company and put our interest in oil and gas wells in that company. Then we sold stock to increase the capital available for developing oil and gas production companies. Typically, the investors would put up $500,000 each for their share of HyTech Industries.

Our record of success in this business had been very good, and it was not difficult to get investors to participate in our new venture. The company was set up in Midland, Texas, where we could hire engineers and management people who were experienced in this part of the energy industry. HyTech did well with leasing prospects on which to drill oil and/or gas wells. Much of this success was due to our employment of very able associates. We not only had the wells, but we built what are called gasoline plants. These plants convert natural gas into liquid gasoline that is stored in large tanks.

HyTech was doing very well financially, but we never had enough capital to put into drilling. I decided that if I could get a public company into which I could merge HyTech, I would accomplish both the matter of having a public company and of not having to go through the process of an initial public offering. Again, I read many annual reports looking for just the right situation. Typical of my prospects was the Cobin Packing Company in Rochester,

New York, which I almost made a deal with. I also negotiated with Arnold Saltzman, who controlled a company called Vista Resources that had a large amount of cash and operated a leather tannery. Saltzman had been an ambassador to one of the Eastern European countries, and was very proud of being called Mr. Ambassador. In the end, Saltzman would not agree to merge HyTech into Vista, but I kept a close watch on Vista from then on, and another opportunity with the company arose a few years later.

The name of the game in the oil and gas industry is money to drill, so I continued to look for other sources of capital as the price of oil began to escalate following the Arab embargo in 1973. But, as I mentioned earlier, when things reached the point that engineering reports were forecasting oil prices would go to $100 a barrel, I felt that it was time to get out of that business and take my profits, which I did. In 1979, the price of oil and gas reached its all-time peak, but it was far less than the figures being used by engineers to sell loans to banks. When the bubble burst, banks lost millions of dollars on oil and gas loans.

The oil and gas boom and bust is a good example of why it is not wise to believe what the experts say when their stories are too good to be true. My activity in the oil and gas business was solely a private agreement between Rex and me and had nothing to do with Fuqua Industries or any of the other public companies with which I was involved. I made some millions from these activities in the 1970s largely due to my good timing in getting in and out of business opportunities.

OTHER BUSINESSES

People often ask what was the most interesting business of the many I have been involved with. That is a hard question to answer because there were several very exciting companies in my portfolio.

We had a company that had a contract with Boeing Aircraft that included our having drawings and descriptions and numbers of the parts for all Boeing airliners. While each airliner in a series may be very similar, the airlines that use the aircraft invariably make modifications. This creates a problem for the airline and for the people who have to service the aircraft. One would think that Boeing would have all of this information itself, but this is the not the way it works in the airliner manufacturing business.

If a Boeing 747 landed in Tokyo and needed a part, the only place where there was an inventory of parts for this particular plane was in our computers. We had a listing of all parts and accessories that might be on any particular Boeing aircraft, and where the part might be in inventory at some other airline or a warehouse somewhere.

Another business that we were involved with at one point was postproduction of motion picture and television programs. In making a movie for theaters, sound effects were all put in after the picture was shot. Often, an actor's voice might not sound natural for some reason in the original taping of a production. It would then become necessary to have the actor watch the taping on a sound stage and rerecord their lines so that the dialogue came out clearer. Actually, a lot of the production in motion pictures for both theaters and television is added after the film has been shot in the field. This process is called postproduction.

The operation of movie theaters was the most profitable business in which I have been involved. It was an all-cash business, there were no accounts receivable, and the only inventory was popcorn, candy and soft drinks. And these were paid for at the end of each month. Most theaters were rented, and that rent was paid at the end of each month. The help was paid usually at the end of a week and, of course, the rental on the movies was paid after they had been shown. Operating a theater was basically a cash business and took less capital than any other business I know.

MISTAKES

Anytime you take risks you're bound to make the wrong decisions sometimes. I could write a book about my mistakes. One that I especially regret happened in 1967 when I messed up a good deal by talking too much.

Since the Saturday afternoon that I first tuned into WRVA Radio in Richmond and caught the Morse code lesson that led to my interest in radio, I had dreamed that I would own WRVA one day. WRVA was owned by Laurus Tobacco Company, which made a well-known brand of pipe tobacco and also owned a television station. I made up my mind to buy Laurus and, after some months of negotiations, we agreed on a price.

I was privately celebrating when I made a major mistake.

I had told the CEO of Laurus that I would continue the operation of his company and allow him to have complete autonomy. He assumed that I meant he would stay in the tobacco business, but while I had made no specific commitment, I intended to sell the tobacco company and keep the radio and television stations.

I was contacted by a competing tobacco company and we had a discussion about their buying Laurus's tobacco business. Unfortunately, they let the word out that they were going to buy Laurus, and it got back to the CEO. So, even though we were well along with the negotiations for the acquisition, the deal was cancelled. I have always regretted this. WRVA was not only the most powerful radio station in Virginia, my home state, but its radio and television stations set the standard for that area, and would have given me much pride and joy. In retrospect, I know that I should not have discussed the deal with the other tobacco company until the acquisition was made. In simple terms, I just goofed.

HOOVER AND AVIS

My attempts to acquire the Hoover Vacuum Cleaner Co. and the Avis Car Rental Co. could be considered mistakes, I suppose. I was convinced that Hoover would be available for acquisition due to the ownership in a control position by members of the Hoover family. I negotiated a price for the control position with the Hoover family members, individually and collectively, but the management did not want the Hoovers to sell the company because they feared they would lose their jobs. That was not necessarily the case — I usually bought companies on the basis of their good management and most of the time left the managers in place.

But even though I had a commitment for a majority of shares of Hoover to be acquired by Fuqua Industries, the management was able to get the takeover matter into the courts. At the trial in Akron, Ohio, our side presented the argument that the Hoover family had already agreed to be bought out, but the company's management rebutted with highly technical legal points. I lost this one because the judge decided that one of the owners I had dealt with was a trustee for a trust that covered the younger members of the Hoover family who were not able to speak for themselves. There was an SEC regulation that provided you could not make an offer in this kind of situation to more than 35 people; otherwise, you had to make a public tender covering all shareholders. By counting the trustee for the younger Hoovers the same as each of the beneficiaries of the trust, the number of people we had contacted exceeded 35. And on that technicality, the judge denied my acquisition of the Hoover Corp.

Avis Car Rental was another company that I tried and failed to acquire. Avis had been a part of ITT and was under the control of a federal trustee who got significant personal income from this source. Of course, the trustee opposed the sale of Avis and we ended up in a federal courtroom in New Jersey.

Our opposition was another conglomerate called Norton-Simon. The CEO of Norton-Simon and I made a private agreement that while in the courtroom we would not change our bid price, so that item was removed from contention. The decision went against us, however, and I have always believed I lost this acquisition opportunity because our lawyer did such a poor job of arguing the case.

I did get some satisfaction out of this effort when I learned that our credit was good enough to support a $100 million unsecured bank loan. Prior to the trial I had gone to Chemical Bank and made a presentation to the president in connection with my application to do the Avis deal. I got a letter the same afternoon committing the bank to the credit line.

CAREER ENTERPRISES

Career Enterprises was a chain of vocational schools that we acquired in 1969 from a Tampa, Florida, entrepreneur named Bill Phillips. The primary educational offerings made by this business were classes for keypunch operators, hotel and motel clerks, and other office-related semiskilled activities.

From an overall perspective, the business looked very profitable. Franchises were sold for $25,000 each to establish a school, and the franchising activity was a major part of the profit picture. We were told that once a franchisee bought one school location, he or she often came back to buy two or three more. The main problem, it turned out, was that, after graduating two or three classes of keypunch operators, the market would become saturated with people having these skills, and a large percentage of the subsequent graduating classes would not be able to find employment. Over time it appeared that the students were being trained for positions where there were no opportunities.

Another problem was the accounting for the sale of a franchise. A franchisee would deposit $5,000 and the bank would loan $20,000, with the loan guaranteed by certificates of deposit of Career Enterprises. As the loan would be paid off over a period of years by the franchisee, the certificates of deposit would be released and Career Enterprises would get the cash. The cost to Career Enterprises of establishing a new franchise location was about $2,500 in cash outlay. Career Enterprises would book as profit the difference between the franchise fee, $25,000, and the out-of-pocket cost of establishing the location for a reported profit of $22,500. When a sufficient number of the schools turned out to be unprofitable and the franchisees were unable to pay off the loans, this profit accounting became a major problem.

We later learned that when Career Enterprises personnel kept the books for the franchisees, the reported profits were on a cash basis that turned out to be misleading. In other words, students would pay their tuition for the course and bills would be paid, although not always punctually, and the franchisee had an initial impression that the school was more profitable than it really was. There were also accusations of misleading advertising to attract prospective students into the schools.

When we discovered the magnitude of the problems, we sent out teams to wind down the franchise system, often fully refunding entire fees to the franchisee. Eventually we sold the business back to Bill Phillips and took a significant write-off.

We later found out that Bill Phillips had been convicted of mail fraud in Texas. What we learned from this experience was the necessity of doing a background check on principals who would be continuing to manage the business they sold to us.

ATLANTA REAL ESTATE

In the early 1970s, I began to buy little pieces of property in and around the area in downtown Atlanta now occupied by Woodruff Park. One day the head of the Trust Company Bank and a prominent Atlanta Realtor made me a proposition to lend me the full price of the real property I had acquired in that area. They said they had a prospect to sell it to when enough property had been acquired and there was no way I could have a loss. I took them at their word, and in a little while I had acquired a substantial amount of property in this area at various prices. The bank put up 100 percent of the money and I had no investment of my own cash. Of course, I had to pay the interest on the money borrowed from the bank. The bank insisted they would not need a mortgage, and that is the key to this lesson.

Near the end of 1974, the bottom dropped out of the real estate market and the C&S Bank found itself in deep trouble with real estate loans. I was summoned to Trust Company and told that C&S had been the prospective buyer for the land I was assembling and that it had changed its mind and no longer wanted to buy the property. I was left with property on my hands that I did not want at a then-market value considerably less than I had paid for it. I offered to give Trust

Company a mortgage on the property, but they declined and told me that I could just pay the interest on the funds they had furnished for the acquisitions. This taught me an expensive lesson: never let a bank lend a full value for high appraisal on property without taking a non-recourse mortgage. If Trust Company had taken mortgages on all of these pieces of property, I simply would have given them the mortgages, said, "Thank you," and walked away from an expensive situation.

VICTIM OF FRAUD

I had rigid rules about due diligence when buying companies. I made sure we examined every legal and financial element of every company. I was most fortunate in not having any serious problems until 1997, when we really had a master fraud put on us. In 1989 Rex and I had paid $12 million cash to an individual for 40 percent of a small public company, Vista Resources, Inc. Vista had a leather manufacturer in Maine, plus about $30 million in cash and no debt. We had to invest in some modernization, but otherwise we bought an ideal financial vehicle that made a good return on what we paid for it. Our plan was to use Vista to acquire other assets and eventually get rid of the leather business because it is an industry that is not followed by security analysts on Wall Street.

We first bought American Southern Insurance Co. in Atlanta for less than $30 million on an installment basis. American Southern turned out about $5 million after-tax profit every year and we were able to get it for a bargain price because the company was being taken over from a fugitive by the Federal Reserve Bank. After several years of operating Vista with the leather business and the insurance business, we decided we would try to get into a growing industry that was consolidating; we bought a small company in Atlanta, Basic American Health Products, a maker of equipment for hospitals and nursing homes.

Meanwhile, we had changed the name from Vista Resources to Fuqua Enterprises, Inc. (FQE), and had the company listed on the New York Stock Exchange. In looking for companies in the health care industry, we came upon Graham-Field Health Products, also listed on the New York Stock Exchange, which was growing at a rapid pace and appeared to have good management. We employed two law firms, Alston & Bird in Atlanta and a Washington firm. Ernst & Young was the auditor for both Fuqua Enterprises and Graham-Field, and we also hired Price Waterhouse-Coopers to represent us in examining the financial records of Graham-Field (GFI).

We made what seemed to me — and I have made a lot of deals — a merger of Fuqua Enterprises (FQE) into GFI on a fair basis for the FQE stockholders. The deal was closed at the end of December 1997. GFI stock had advanced from about $12 to almost $20 in the six-month period we had been working on the deal. Rex and I and our several family accounts would own about 30 percent of the shares of GFI. When GFI was late in putting out their 1997 financials, we sensed something was wrong. Indeed it turned out that GFI had been falsifying financial data for three years. GFI had never made a profit but they had very cleverly concealed this from their auditors, Ernst & Young, and Price Waterhouse had not detected the falsification of the books. Rex and I are embarrassed about the whole thing. Never had I been the victim of a major fraud. This situation is tied up in litigation with several lawsuits in progress and Graham-Field is in bankruptcy. Of course, Rex and I have lost the $12 million cash we paid for our 40 percent control position in Vista in 1989, but we have swallowed our loss and moved on.

PART V

FRIENDS AT THE WHITE HOUSE AND BEYOND

CHAPTER 15

POLITICS & POWER

In politics I was and am a Democrat. Perhaps I should be classified as a conservative Democrat. I know that I have been better off personally when we have had Democrats in the White House. I think they have had a long-term commitment to policies that are most beneficial to all Americans. The Democratic Party is the party of inclusion, for it addresses the interests of average working families, as well as the affluent. Democrats brought the nation Social Security, Medicare, deposit insurance, and many other programs that benefit a majority of the population. But let me make clear that I am an American who will not let his political leanings prevent an alliance with the Republicans when they have programs that I think are best for our country.

When I entered politics in the 1950s, I did so as a Democrat.

There were few Republicans in the state government in Georgia at the time, so I would have been ineffective and lonely as a Republican. My opportunity to get into state politics came about when the man representing Richmond County in the Georgia House decided to run for mayor of Augusta. He resigned from the House in order to devote all of his energy to the mayoral campaign, and all the candidates who announced they were going to run for his unexpired term were young lawyers. I decided that there ought to be somebody representing the district who was not in the legal profession.

I qualified for the 1957 Democratic primary — there was no Republican opposition — and beat the socks off the others. I had opposition in maybe one election after that. But since I had funded recreation programs for blacks in Augusta and had a reputation as a candidate who supported equal rights, I had the backing of all the black voters, and I had enough prestige that nobody could whip me.

I enjoyed my years in politics, but this was a turbulent time because of the burgeoning Civil Rights Movement. The old county unit system, which gave sparsely populated rural counties as much representation as the larger counties, had been declared illegal and a new political order was on the rise.

I saw the entire history of Georgia change in one sitting of the House of Representatives in 1958. Marvin Griffin was governor and he had handpicked his successor — or so he thought. In that era, elections were often run and candidates elected based on how strongly they supported the building of rural roads. This was important because, under the County

Unit System, every voter in the rural areas visualized a paved road coming by his house.

Marvin's choice for his successor was Roger H. Lawson, a man from Hawkinsville who was chairman of the State Highway Board. Lawson was so sure of his election that he had already moved his office from the Capitol to a room in one of the hotels. Lawson didn't think he needed to campaign very much because he was confident that Marvin Griffin would pass the latest rural road bill and that would ensure his election.

The bill had been the subject of conversation among representatives for several weeks, but Marvin thought he had everything lined up so there would be little opposition. On the day the bill came up, Representative Frank Cheatham of Savannah, who sat next to me in the House, got up and yelled, "Mr. Speaker, Mr. Speaker!" Marvin Moats, speaker of the House, thought that Cheatham was for the bill and simply wanted to make some observation about procedure. He would not have recognized him had he realized Cheatham was not only against Marvin Griffin, but was ready to do anything to ensure the defeat of Griffin's candidate in the governor's race. Once he was recognized, Cheatham asked if he could come to the podium, a request that was always honored as a courtesy. Representative Cheatham was a polio victim and walked on two crutches. I can see him now as he moved between the seats to the outside aisle and proceeded on his crutches to the front of the House. By the time he got to the podium, there was dead silence. Everyone had been anticipating with curiosity what this representative had on his mind, never dreaming it would be something that would eliminate Griffin's candidate as his successor.

When Cheatham got to the podium, he simply asked for a deferment of action until Monday (this was Friday) so that everyone would have a chance to go home and discuss the bill with their constituents. This was something that gave everyone a tremendous amount of relief; tensions were so high because of the power Griffin wielded as governor that any delay in having to cast a vote for or against him was welcome. Of course the House approved this resolution and the whole matter was delayed until Monday morning. Over the weekend, the majority of the representatives gained the courage to vote against the bill and that was the end of Marvin Griffin's influence on the governorship. Lawson later withdrew from the race with the excuse that he was "not well enough known."

The bill before the House had been for $50 million in bonds to build roads in the rural areas, but the governor or a candidate for governor could turn it into promises of $500 million. This was basically pork barrel legislation that allowed unnecessary spending of money to build roads where none were needed, simply to increase the political clout of the governor or state highway commissioner. This had been a very powerful tool in Georgia politics, yet that one episode spelled the end of it. Ernest Vandiver was then elected governor and, with his administration, the rural road business passed into history.

When Carl Sanders was elected governor in 1962, he wanted to make some important changes in State House offices and the job of hatchet man fell on me. I'll never forget the day I had to tell George L. Smith, who was Speaker of the House, that he wouldn't have that job anymore. It was a difficult assignment for me, because George L. Smith had become perhaps my closest friend in the House of Representatives. But he understood, as did others who were similarly affected by a change in the administration. Still, it was not an easy thing for me to do.

There were other incidents during that time that I got a laugh out of, however. Peter Zack Geer was elected lieutenant governor at the same time Sanders was elected governor, and Carl wanted to be sure he had the loyalty of Geer and other officials. Since Sanders had tremendous power as governor (a situation that no longer exists), he could have a great deal of influence on other departments through the budget process. Carl was concerned about Geer, so after the election he asked him to come to Augusta where they could have a heart-to-heart talk about whether Peter Zack was going to be loyal to the governor and back his legislative programs. To make sure that Peter Zack would not renege on his promises, we secretly tape-recorded our meeting at my office at WJBF television. In those days there were no miniature tape recorders, so I took one of the TV station's machines, put it in a little powder room in my office, and disguised the microphone. This was the type of hardball politics that was done at that time.

The same thing is practiced today in politics, but perhaps in a more sophisticated manner.

One of the most exciting events in my political career occurred in 1966 when those of us in the Legislature were called upon to decide who the next governor was going to be. Neither Bo Callaway nor Lester Maddox had received a majority vote and therefore, according to the state constitution, the Legislature was required to elect the governor.

We decided the fair way to do this was for the members of the Legislature to vote according to how their district voted. Since most of the counties outside of the metropolitan areas were very strong in their support for Lester Maddox, it was a foregone conclusion that he would be elected. Ironically, Maddox was the first governor to move into a new governor's mansion that I had been instrumental in getting built in Atlanta in 1967 — and which he himself had vehemently opposed.

DRIVE-IN BANKING WINDOWS

When I was in the Georgia House and Senate, a committee chairman had a great deal of influence on whether a bill (proposed legislation) would live or die. I was chairman of the Banking Committee in the House and later, when I was in the Senate, I was also chairman of this important committee. In February 1959, a bill was introduced that would allow banks to have drive-in windows within 1,000 feet of the main banking building. In those days, the legislature more or less micromanaged competition in the banking business. Banks were not allowed to have a drive-in window unless it was attached to the main banking building. If the bill were passed, banks would be able to have a branch of a sort within about a quarter mile of the main bank building, and this would allow banks to give better service to their customers. You cannot imagine how controversial this proposal was, even though it is laughable today.

To avoid a huge debate on the floor, which inevitably would have bruised feelings on both sides of the question, I decided the solution was just not to let the bill come up. I gave it a "pocket veto" by simply not calling any hearing or letting the bill go any further. The House passed a resolution ordering that I be "brought to the floor" and caused to disgorge the bill. I hid out in my hotel room for most of one day so as not to be found. Eventually, I knew that the best thing to do would be to let the bill go to the floor, so I released it. The House, by divided vote, passed the bill allowing drive-in windows — or the "despicable branches" — to be built near the main bank buildings.

When I first went into the House of Representatives in 1957, a bank could not take a deposit or cash a check except in its main office, and there were many similar restrictions that prevented these institutions from giving better service to their customers. In the eight years I was in the House and Senate, I helped bring about a gradual relaxation of these restrictions through the authorship of successively more lenient banking regulations.

THE GOVERNOR'S MANSION

One of the most satisfying things I achieved while in politics was getting a new governor's mansion built for the people of Georgia. The old mansion was located in midtown Atlanta in the historic neighborhood of Ansley Park, close to the Piedmont Driving Club. It was an ancient, gray, stone building that was not very well maintained.

When I was elected to the legislature, I had an opportunity to see what the mansion really looked like inside and it was not pretty. The carpets were worn and stained, and in some places dogs had left smelly evidence of their presence. The roof leaked, and when it rained, the staff had to put buckets in various places to catch the water. It was an unbelievable situation. Of course, the public had no way of knowing what the mansion really looked like, because very few people had any reason to go there.

I thought it was necessary that the symbol of the state of Georgia be repaired or a new mansion be built, and I was determined to get this project off the ground. I began to talk to various political leaders, who all admitted we needed a new mansion, but who all said, "You know we can't build a new governor's mansion in Georgia because the people would never stand for that kind of expense. They would think it was a waste of money because they don't know the terrible condition of the building." But I could get things done in any sort of organization, and I felt that there would be a way to get the money.

At that time, we had a State Building Authority that

owned office buildings and other property the state used. If I could get the governor's mansion to be considered a state office building, I thought, that might be a way for us to get a new mansion. I consulted with Secretary of State Ben Fortson, who was one of the keenest people in the political arena, and he agreed that technically there was no reason the mansion couldn't be owned by the State Building Authority. Under the existing system, office buildings and other properties were leased to the state and rent was paid by the government to the State Building Authority. This organization could also issue bonds to finance any new office buildings. Bonds were issued for each project with a corresponding resolution from the legislature providing for rent, which would exactly pay off the principal and interest of the bonds.

Ben Fortson gave me a great deal of encouragement, and his help proved to be important as I went through this process. I next contacted George L. Smith, who was Speaker of the House. He agreed that we needed a new mansion and that few members of the House would be opposed to an outright issuance of state funds, but he believed, of course, that no one would vote for it out of fear of backlash. Lieutenant Governor Garland T. Byrd also said it was a much-needed project and offered me his full cooperation. Governor Ernest Vandiver, who was living in the old governor's mansion, was 100 percent in favor of the effort and thought it would be a good investment for the state, but he too did not want to be associated with the project publicly. However, he promised to help me if I could get the State

Building Authority Act amended so that he would not have to sign it as an appropriation for the mansion. In other words, he would do anything to help as long as he didn't have to commit himself directly.

I asked Governor Vandiver if he had any objections to the Legislature authorizing a commission to "study" the need for a new mansion and to recommend that it be authorized. I also got him to agree that I would suggest the names of those who would be on the commission, since I felt it was my project. The first job of the study committee was to select a site to build a new mansion and/or to buy a suitable existing house. We looked at a number of sites and houses, and decided on a piece of property that was owned by Robert F. Maddox, a former mayor of Atlanta who had developed the First National Bank. Mr. Maddox was 91 and we were not sure what his reaction would be to our buying his acreage on the east side of West Paces Ferry Road.

My plan was to amend the State Building Authority so that the new mansion could be included in the things the department could own. It was not called the governor's mansion in the legislation, by the way, but had a nice camouflaged name: "an executive center." We decided to add this amendment to the Building Authority Act during what is called "the period of unanimous consent." This was a device used in Georgia to enable counties to pass legislation applying only to a particular county or city without going through the entire legislative process. Certain days of the week were reserved for it, and much legislative business was therefore handled efficiently and did not take up the time of the members of the Senate and House, even though it had all the authority of a full vote by both legislative bodies.

I brought the bill up in the House and, of course, being in the spirit of unanimous consent, it was adopted by the entire House of Representatives. However, nobody knew what they were voting for. The process was repeated in the Senate. It was quite some time before the newspapers caught on to the fact that the House and Senate had appropriated money to authorize and increase the bonding limits of the State Building Authority.

CARL SANDERS

"If the appropriations bill for the governor's mansion had been listed as a separate item, we never would have been able to get the money to build it. We knew the bill would create a furor in the General Assembly and with the public, so J. B. and the state auditor, Edmund Thrasher, figured out a way to hide it. If you go back and look at the appropriations bill for that year, you can't find any mention of the governor's mansion."

I was one of the members of the committee who engaged the architect and made the basic decisions that a property owner would have to make if the building were a private residence. At one point the project almost failed because the price Mr. Maddox wanted for his property was more than the amount of money we had provided for in the amendment. Fortunately, a $40,000 gift from Mills Lane, the president of Citizens and Southern National Bank, saved the day. Lane was on the study committee along with others of my friends.

I had hoped that we could get the mansion built in time for Carl Sanders to move into it while he was governor. However, construction and various delays made that impossible, so in 1967 the first occupant of the new governor's mansion was Lester Maddox, who was no relation to Robert Maddox.

Among the delays we had was a shortage of funds. The amendment to the State Building Authority provided only $1 million for the project, but with the cooperation of Ben Fortson, we found a way to put another $1 million in the pot. That gave us $2 million and allowed us to complete the project.

CARL SANDERS

"The new mansion has served the state of Georgia tremendously. We collected furniture through gifts and some state appropriations, but the items we put in cost less than $600,000. Governor Roy Barnes said recently that the furniture now is appraised for $14 million or more."

The lesson of the governor's mansion is that where there's a will, there's a way in almost all ventures, whether public or private. The new building has been a remarkably good investment. Succeeding governors have used it to entertain heads of state and industrial prospects for new industries in Georgia, as well as for various social events. I am glad I had the opportunity to make this project happen. I not only did a service to the state, but I got a great deal of personal pride in having accomplished this mission.

WHERE THERE'S SMOKE...

There's a popular idea that much political horse-trading in this country is done in "smoke-filled rooms" rather than formally in the Legislature. This is really true in many instances. When I was in the Georgia House and Senate, much of the important legislation was decided on the top floor of the Henry Grady Hotel. The Henry Grady was a 14-story hotel that stood on the corner of Peachtree and International Boulevard. (It has since been replaced by the Peachtree Plaza Hotel.) The most important room in the Henry Grady Hotel from a political standpoint was 1420. Members of the House and Senate met in this room every Sunday night for drinks, sometimes food, and always a discussion of legislative matters and politics in general. That was before smoking became unpopular and prohibited, and, indeed, the room was filled with smoke.

I had a room on the 14th floor at the Henry Grady that I arranged for when I was elected to the Legislature after I learned that this was where the political leaders stayed when they were in Atlanta for the legislative session. It was a good investment, as I got off to good relations from the start with the political leaders of Georgia.

My years in the Georgia House and Senate were never dull because there were so many colorful characters. One of the most interesting fellows was a representative from a small south Georgia county who had only one arm. This gentleman was very vocal in his opposition to a measure allowing the sale of mixed drinks, even though it was clear that a majority of the House favored the bill.

Finally, word got around that on a certain day, we would get this fellow out of the way, take a quick vote, and pass the mixed drink bill. It was set up so that this representative would be told that he had an appointment at 2 o'clock with Jim Gillis, the Highway Commissioner and a very powerful man in state government. He was told that Gillis had summoned him because he wanted to talk to him about a road he was interested in. The plan worked well up to a point. Gillis did summon the representative, and he did leave the chamber to go across the street to see "Mr. Jim," as Gillis was called. While he was gone, we went through all of the motion to clearing the way to pass the mixed drink bill. We were just about to take the vote when, somehow, the representative sitting across the street suddenly had the strange feeling that he'd been taken.

I can see it like it was yesterday. He rushed into the chamber, waving his one arm and yelling loudly enough to be heard all the way downtown, "Mr. Speaker, Mr. Speaker!" He interrupted the proceedings and demanded that he be allowed to speak. Of course, he couldn't be denied so he made his usual speech against the evils of mixed drinks, and that was the end of the bill for that period.

CHAPTER 16

RACE RELATIONS, THE KENNEDYS, AND THE GOVERNORSHIP

The 1960s ushered in a new wave of political leaders in the South, and my friend Carl Sanders and I were in the forefront. Almost all the members of the Georgia delegation to the 1960 Democratic Convention were new because previous delegates had always been named by the Herman Talmadge and Marvin Griffin side of Georgia politics, whereas this group was appointed by the more progressive governor Ernest Vandiver.

We left for Los Angeles with the intention of voting for Lyndon Johnson, but when we arrived it became clear that John F. Kennedy had the Democratic nomination locked up before the convention opened. There was a Kennedy waiting to greet us at the airport, and there was a Kennedy meeting with every state delegation. It seemed as if the Kennedys had every rental car in Los Angeles.

Those of us in the Georgia delegation soon realized that a vote for Lyndon Johnson was a wasted gesture. Although we still wanted to go for LBJ all the way, we shifted our votes to Kennedy when it became obvious that LBJ had no chance of becoming the Democratic nominee. The horse trading that went on before the Kennedys announced that LBJ was their choice for vice president was interesting, since it was widely known that Johnson and the Kennedys disliked each other. JFK knew, however, that he had to have Johnson on the ticket if he wanted to have any chance of carrying the South. This decision had been thought out carefully by Jack Kennedy and the huge Kennedy clan before they went to LBJ and offered him the nomination, but it still stunned many of the delegates.

I had several occasions to meet with Jack Kennedy after he became president, and I liked him very much. After Carl Sanders became governor in the early 1960s, we were constantly alert to the possibility of any racial disturbances in Georgia, such as the ones that were erupting in Mississippi, Alabama, and other Southern states. Feelings were running high about the Civil Rights Bill at that time, and we wanted to head off any violence before it started. We knew if we could get the FBI involved to warn us about any simmering problems or Klan activity, we had enough local contacts in most places in Georgia to stop it before it got worse. When we asked President Kennedy if he could get the FBI to help, he told us he thought it was a good idea. He suggested that we talk to his brother Bobby about it since Bobby was the attorney general and head of the Justice Department.

I vividly recall my visit with the attorney general. He was sitting on a small sofa eating a sandwich when I arrived, and he asked me to sit by him while he finished his lunch. I explained what we wanted the Justice Department to do and he then called in Nicholas Katzenbach, the assistant attorney general in charge of civil rights matters, and outlined our proposal to him. After we finished our visit, it was clear that Bobby wanted to talk to somebody and I was the nearest person who would listen. He told me while we were sitting right there on the sofa what President Kennedy had gone through to get the civil rights legislation passed. He described the frustrations they had had with every approach they had used to try to get Congress to act. Bobby became very emotional at this point, and big tears rolled down his cheeks. It was clear that he had his whole heart in the civil rights legislation. Anyone who says that the Kennedys were not sincere in their desire to improve relations between whites and blacks never had the experience with them that I had.

Between Governor Sanders, myself, and our friends, we were able to stifle every prospective disturbance and incident in Georgia that the FBI believed would become serious. This was extremely helpful and kept us from having the troubles most other Southern states had. I was always very grateful to Bobby Kennedy for what he had agreed to do. And of course I felt a sense of gratitude to President John Kennedy for the kind way in which he had treated me.

Jack Kennedy proved helpful on another occasion when Carl Sanders and I learned that the Army was planning to move the Signal Corps from Fort Gordon in Augusta to Fort Monmouth in New Jersey.

CARL SANDERS

"I had not taken office yet, but I immediately contacted Senator Richard Russell, who was the chairman of the Armed Services Committee, and asked him if he couldn't help me get that order reversed. He said he couldn't do anything about it, so J. B. and I flew to Washington to see Jack Kennedy. We told him that closing the fort would be devastating to the economy of Augusta."

After Carl and I made our case, we witnessed something that proved we were truly in the office of the most powerful man in the country, if not the world. Kennedy picked up the telephone and asked the operator to get him somebody in the Pentagon. He then told this person that if they were planning to shut down or move Fort Gordon, the decision must be reversed. Carl and I were two happy individuals when we got in my airplane and flew back to Augusta. In due course, nothing was done to threaten Fort Gordon, and the power of the commanding officer of the military had been demonstrated to us.

Not many people know this, but I was actually responsible

for uninviting President Kennedy to come to Atlanta once during this volatile period. Some people think that one event might have changed the course of history.

It was August 1963 and I had just seen an article in the *Atlanta Constitution* that President Kennedy had agreed to come to Georgia Tech to speak at the college's 75th anniversary. Well, this was at the height of the debate in Congress over the Civil Rights Bill, and there was a lot of tension in the South. I called Governor Sanders and told him we couldn't allow President Kennedy to come to Atlanta, since there might be trouble because of all the bitterness over the bill. Carl said, "How are we going to stop him?" I said, "We'll have to uninvite him," and Carl said, "I'm not going to do it." So I told him I would take care of it.

I was chairman of the state Democratic Party at that time, so I called Kennedy's chief of staff, Kenneth O'Donnell, and set up an appointment. I told him I wanted to come in the back door instead of through the room where all the press people were, and I didn't want my name listed on the guest book. He agreed, so I flew up to Washington and went in quietly through the back door. After Kennedy and I exchanged a few pleasantries, I told him about the problem I saw with his visit in light of the Civil Rights Bill. The last thing Carl Sanders and I wanted was for something to happen while he was in Atlanta. I put it on a largely political basis. I told him that any embarrassments or incidents in Georgia might indicate that he was not popular in the South, and that from a purely political standpoint this could be embarrassing for him. He readily accepted my judgment, and called in his press secretary Pierre Salinger and told him to work out a cancellation. Salinger later announced that due to "changed circumstances," the president would not visit Atlanta.

I thought I had pulled the whole thing off without anybody knowing of my involvement, but a Washington reporter for the *Atlanta Journal* began checking around and discovered that my name was on the visitors' books of two of the Georgia congressmen I had seen while I was in town. She asked me if I had been responsible for getting Kennedy not to come. I didn't lie, but I did say something like, "I don't believe it would be appropriate for the Democratic chairman to do that. As Democratic chairman, I would always be glad to see the President come to Georgia. I hope that he will find another occasion to come to this state."

Looking back now, I hate to think what might have happened if the President had come to Atlanta that August. There was so much hatred among the virulently anti-integration elements of Georgia and the South that summer of 1963. I have the very strong feeling that we could have had the November tragedy of Dallas right here in Georgia.

When I was running Carl Sanders's campaign for governor in 1962, race was of course a hot political issue. I recall one particular meeting on a Saturday afternoon on Auburn Avenue with those considered to be the leaders of the black community. Martin Luther King Jr. was in jail in Albany, Georgia, at the time, and although he had been cleared of any charges, he refused to leave the jail. This created a particularly bad situation for the Sanders campaign because the supporters of Sanders's opponent, Marvin Griffin, had been playing the race card, claiming that Sanders was behind King's participation in the demonstrations that had torn Albany apart. King had intentionally gotten arrested to bring national attention to the situation, but Marvin Griffin's camp was using the incident to suggest that we were involved in keeping MLK Jr. in jail.

I remember Martin Luther King Sr. telling me, in what I believe was all sincerity, that he had no control over his son and was very much disturbed that the younger King wanted to stay in jail. The situation was finally resolved when Attorney General Bobby Kennedy made a call to Martin Luther King Jr. in Albany and convinced him to withdraw from the demonstrations in Albany by leaving jail.

The division over race grew even greater after President Kennedy was assassinated in 1963 and Lyndon Johnson took office. As head of the state Democratic Party, I appointed Leroy Johnson as the first black delegate to the Democratic convention in 1964. And, because of my position, I was in charge of LBJ's campaign when he ran against Goldwater that year.

I had several debates with Joe Tribble, a lawyer from Savannah who was the Republican Party chairman for Georgia. We would meet in some rural areas and debate the candidacies of LBJ and Barry Goldwater. The audiences would boo and whistle and do all kinds of things to embarrass me when I was speaking.

CARL SANDERS

"It was a very volatile time in politics when they were trying to get the Civil Rights Bill passed, and we took a helluva lot of heat when we supported LBJ in 1964. J. B. and I were about the only people who would have anything to do with Johnson or Hubert Humphrey when they came to the state. Senator Richard Russell went to Spain, supposedly to inspect military bases, and Senator Herman Talmadge went underground. Of course, once Lyndon Johnson was elected, Georgia got tremendous benefits from his administration in the form of federal money and grants."

The feelings in Georgia were so bitter against Lyndon Johnson because of his support of the Civil Rights Bill that people who knew me wouldn't speak to me on the street. Our children suffered all kinds of abuse at school because their daddy was for Johnson. I recall going into a restaurant in Augusta, and as I walked down the aisle to a booth, I heard somebody say, "There goes that S.O.B." It was a rough time for us.

DOTTIE FUQUA

"We had many difficult times over J. B.'s position on racial matters. When we were living in Augusta in the early '60s, there was to be a home tour for the garden club and the chairman called and said, 'Mrs. Fuqua, some black officers from Fort Gordon have bought tickets to go on the tour and some of the ladies say they refuse to open their homes if they come. What are your feelings?' I told her my husband represents everyone in the county and the black officers can come as my guests. Some of them drove by, but no one stopped. Some of the ladies said they would have refused to let them in."

I suppose I became a liberal with regard to race relations because of my experiences growing up in a part of the South where blacks were not treated much differently than they must have been in the days of slavery. Under the sharecropping system, a farmer would make an arrangement with a landowner whereby he was to receive a share of any profits. Unfortunately, there were white farmers who would take advantage of black farmers who either were illiterate or did not have enough education to calculate what their true share of the crop might be. For example, blacks often were at a disadvantage when it came to such things as the cost of fertilizer. An uneducated black man might not be able to determine how much fertilizer was used and what the cost was. The same thing applied to materials or services that were secured for a crop from third parties. When the tobacco crop was sold, the black sharecropper was ultimately at the mercy of the white farmer.

This is not to suggest that all sharecropping was unfair to the black man — Papa was as fair and honest in his dealings with the blacks as any white farmer I ever knew of. But there were a considerable number of dishonest practices going on when I was growing up in Virginia, and the black man was at a distinct disadvantage. There was no such thing as time off for vacations for black people on the farms, and they were totally dependent upon the attitude of the white "bossman." I do not recall a single instance in those days where a black man got a paid vacation.

The unequal treatment of blacks and whites was most evident in the school system. When I was a youth, the education of black children usually extended only to three or four grades. The black children walked to school because there were no appropriations for transportation for them and because, of course, blacks and whites were not allowed to ride the same buses. It was just the way things were. Blacks were considered inferior and were not allowed in white churches, white schools or white restaurants. Everything was segregated by race, including water fountains and restrooms.

Since that time, much has changed for blacks, but not as rapidly as you might think. In 1974, when Lady Bird Johnson wanted to bring Lucille Ball to Atlanta for the premiere of "Mame" as a political fund-raiser for a memorial park honoring Lyndon Johnson, the city's most prestigious private clubs refused our request for a reception. Their reason was that some of the Secret Service agents were black and therefore would not be welcome in the club. An unspoken reason was that Maynard Jackson had been elected the first black mayor of Atlanta and he, of course, would have been one of the invited guests. Neither the Piedmont Driving Club nor the Capital City Club would let us have the reception, so we ended up holding it at Phipps Plaza.

I can't explain why I felt differently from some other Southern whites about blacks. Maybe it is because of the example of fairness that Papa set when I was at a young and impressionable age. But I just knew that everyone should have the same opportunities, no matter what color his or her skin was.

CHAPTER 17

JIMMY CARTER'S FIRST ELECTION

The Democratic Party chairman of Georgia during the 1960s was a very influential position. The chairman was a liaison between the governor and the state government on the one hand, and the federal government on the other. I could go to Washington and see Cabinet members or anybody else in the federal government, which was Democratic during my administration.

The chairman of the party, up to and through my stint from 1962 to 1966, had to be a person of substantial means because of the way politics ran in Georgia then. There was no established Republican Party, so there was little financial support for Republican candidates, and therefore no Republican primary. Primaries had to be financed by the party, and a statewide primary was quite expensive. At one point during my tenure as chairman, I was on the hook for the party for about $200,000 for the statewide primaries.

The perks of the party chairman, though, were considerable. If someone did the governor or the party some particular favor, I could reward them by getting them on one of the Department of Commerce foreign trips that seemed to be in abundance. I was asked about various federal appointments and was in a position to do a number of people nice favors. For example, I could arrange for a lawyer to be named by the federal government or one of the federal agencies to represent the agency on some matter that concerned Georgia.

The party rules at that time gave the chairman very considerable authority to act on political matters. That power proved to be influential in launching the career of a peanut farmer from South Georgia.

A few weeks after the 1962 Democratic primary, Carl Sanders and I had been invited to go to South Dakota on the Coca-Cola plane to shoot pheasants. The plane dropped us back off in Augusta on Saturday afternoon.

It was the 3rd of November, 1962, and the general election, which was just a formality since Democrats had no Republican opposition in those days, was held on the 6th of November, the following Tuesday. When I got to my house on Park Avenue in Augusta, Dottie told me there was a man in the living room who had been waiting for two hours for me to come home.

The visitor was Charles Kirbo, an attorney with the prominent Atlanta law firm of King and Spalding, who said he was representing Jimmy Carter in an election dispute. At that time, Carter was a virtual unknown in state politics, and he had run into trouble with Joe Hurst, a longtime political boss in Quitman County. Carter was running against Hurst's handpicked candidate, Homer Moore, and Hurst was upset that the recent redistricting had joined six rural Georgia counties with the more populous Sumter County. Moore had won the Democratic primary before the district was redrawn, but with the formation of the new district, his election was considered invalid and a new primary had been held on October 16.

Kirbo explained that Carter had been defeated in the new primary because of a number of election irregularities. The polling place in Quitman County had been moved to the Ordinary's office so that Hurst could greet voters while handing them their ballots. There were no voting booths, so Hurst had arranged for the ballot box to be placed on a small table. When voters approached the table, he slid Moore's campaign card onto the table and stared at the voters as they marked their ballots. From time to time, Kirbo claimed, Hurst reached into the ballot box to remove any ballots that were not marked to his liking.

There were other influences on the voters as well, Kirbo said, including the fact that Hurst's wife was the Welfare Director for the county, and Hurst delivered the welfare checks himself. In addition to being a state legislator, he drew a second salary as an employee of the State Agriculture Department and controlled many jobs in the community.

When the votes were tallied, there were 100 more votes than the 327 who had voted in Quitman County. With the help of Kirbo, Carter demanded and got a recount of the voters on November 1, five days before the general election. Kirbo reported that when the box was opened, they found a separate wad of 150 votes for Moore, all listed in alphabetical order. Many of the voters had been dead for years. Carter was declared the winner of the state primary by 65 votes, but there was still another hurdle to clear. In order for the change to be valid, I had to certify the results and get the papers back to Secretary of State Ben Fortson before the general election. Since the general election was only three days away, I didn't see how this would be possible. Kirbo insisted that he would go back to Atlanta and deliver the certification to Fortson and then he and other friends of Jimmy Carter would go from one precinct to another and change by hand all the ballots that had been printed.

Being in the House of Representatives myself, I knew some of the characters in the county that was the most highly populated in the senatorial district in which Carter was running. I basically was leaning toward changing the nominee to Carter, but I decided I had to find Carl Sanders, who had been nominated for governor in the same primary, and ask his opinion. I found Sanders in the barber shop and I explained to him what was going on in my house between Kirbo and myself and asked him what he wanted me to do. Sanders said it was my decision.

I had never heard of Jimmy Carter before this incident,

but I finally agreed to Kirbo's pleas and signed the certification. Kirbo then asked me if I would call the operator of the charter plane service at Daniel Field and vouch for him as a good credit risk to rent a plane. I did so and when he returned to Atlanta, he went immediately to Ben Fortson's house and on Sunday he and Carter had the ballot changed.

Now, one can look at this incident and say that I was responsible for Jimmy Carter being elected to his first public office and that I in effect made him a state senator. Indeed, that is true. Look at all the things we can put down in the "What If?" column. If I had not gotten back from South Dakota, I would not have been available to change the outcome of the primary. If I had not agreed to listen to Kirbo's pleas, Carter would not have been elected state senator. Although I really did influence Carter's political career in the beginning, his record speaks for itself from then on. But Jimmy Carter himself has told the story of his start in politics many times, including in his first book *Why Not the Best?*

In the fall of 1975, Jimmy Carter came to my office to tell me about his future political plans and to ask for my help. When I asked him what he intended to do, he said, "I'm going to be president." I thought that he might be taking a job as president of some company, so I asked him, "Jimmy, president of what?" And Carter replied, "I'm going to be president of the United States." Needless to say, I was startled.

When I pointed out that he was no longer governor and had no forum to use in running for national office, he outlined step-by-step how he would begin with the Iowa Caucus and go from state to state to run in each primary. He said he planned to do this using a small organization. It was a logical sequence he related, but even though I knew he was sincere, I thought it was all a joke. When we finished our conversation, I decided I would flatter him by taking him around the office and introducing him to several of our corporate officers as "the next president of the United States." After he had left the office, there was much laughter about Jimmy Carter becoming the next president, but he knew what he wanted and how to get it. I have the greatest admiration for people who have that kind of determination.

When Carter was president, Dottie and I were invited to the White House for a State dinner in which the honoree was Margaret Thatcher, the prime minister of the United Kingdom. Carter himself introduced me to Mrs. Thatcher and told her that I was responsible for his being president.

I take no credit or blame for Jimmy Carter becoming president of the United States — all I did was influence his career on his way up. Jimmy Carter became president in only 14 years from the time he was elected to the state Senate, a feat that no other president has achieved. He went from being a peanut farmer to becoming state senator and governor of Georgia and winning the election as president in 1976.

Jimmy Carter and I have remained friends through all these years. While many of his friends were disappointed in his performance as president, no one can criticize his accomplishments since he retired from politics. He has indeed been the best ex-president we ever had.

CHAPTER 18

LYNDON JOHNSON, A LONGTIME FRIEND

Of all the famous people I have known, including several U.S. presidents, Lyndon Johnson was my closest friend. I visited him frequently on his ranch in Texas after he left the White House, and I saw a side of LBJ that few others saw. My first visit to his ranch was in 1962 following the Democratic primary in Georgia. Since there was no Republican Party in Georgia, Carl Sanders had in effect been elected governor in the primary, and LBJ had invited Sanders, along with Governor Ernest Vandiver, Senator Richard Russell, and myself, to deer hunt.

When we got to the ranch, we split up in two cars and I rode all day with LBJ. As the sun was setting, LBJ realized that everybody else in the party had gotten a buck except me. He promised me he was going to make sure I got a deer. I was embarrassed, so I tried to talk him out of this by explaining that we had to leave early the following morning. I made every excuse I could think of so as not to have to go hunting again, but he would have none of it.

Before we went to bed, LBJ told me that we would get up early the next morning and that he and I would go find a deer for me to shoot. Sure enough, at 5 o'clock Johnson awakened me and Carl Sanders, who was sleeping in the same room, and hustled us out to get my deer.

We first went to a neighbor's ranch and had breakfast, then we began looking for a suitable buck for me to bag. It was clear LBJ wasn't going to let me leave the ranch until I had gotten one. It was a matter of pride for him as the host. He told me that he had never had a guest who didn't get a deer, including President Kennedy.

All the bucks must have been listening, because it seemed that suddenly there were none to be found. Eventually, we came across a fair specimen of a male deer with antlers. Unfortunately, Johnson had made me so nervous that I could hardly load the gun, much less aim it.

CARL SANDERS

"I remember the deer hunt quite well. I had killed a deer earlier and Lyndon Johnson was not going to let us quit hunting until J. B. got one. J. B. shot five or six times using my back as a base to hold the rifle, and he finally got his deer. Whenever we were on LBJ's ranch we hunted in Lincoln Continental automobiles."

No one was happier than LBJ and more relieved than I when I killed that deer. We could finally leave the ranch, even though it was several hours later than we planned. A few weeks later, LBJ sent me the mounted head of my prize and I still have it hanging at my hunting lodge.

Some of the best times I spent with LBJ were after he left the White House on those mornings when it would just be the two of us at his table. We would sit there after breakfast and he would entertain me with stories from his political career. He kept a telephone on the table and one day we were sitting there when LBJ received a call from President Nixon telling him he had appointed John Connally as Secretary of the Treasury. Connally was a former governor of Texas who had been wounded in the Dallas motorcade in which President Kennedy had been shot and killed, and he had been like a son to LBJ. Johnson's face turned red as he talked and when he hung up he was furious that Connally had not called him first. This was a shocking thing for Johnson to accept, and for the next two days he kept muttering that Connally shouldn't have done that to him. He had no respect for people who switched from the Democratic Party to the Republican side, and he saw them as opportunists.

Johnson was always the perfect host, in spite of his health problems and bouts of depression. He had a remarkable collection of exotic animals that people from all over the world had given him, and he was always anxious to show them off to his guests. LBJ loved to take me for rides on his ranch and around his neighbors' ranches. Usually he drove a four-door Lincoln convertible, and he ignored the speed limits. One of his favorite "toys" was an amphibious vehicle. He got a big kick out of loading his friends in it, driving down to a lake and going right into the water, much to the delight and astonishment of his guests.

Having the Secret Service around all the time really irritated LBJ, and he would use any means to try to get away from them. When we were driving around the ranches, he would often pick up the microphone on his two-way radio and tell the Secret Service to stay back after they opened a gate to go from one pasture to another. "I'll be back in a little while," he told them. "Y'all just stay where you are." It did no good, because as soon as we began to disappear, the Secret Service car would pull up close enough to keep us in sight and see what we were doing.

I was visiting LBJ at his ranch a month before he died when he took me down to the cemetery where his body would be buried. As we stood there, he described in considerable detail how his funeral would be conducted. When I went to the funeral in January 1973, I had already seen the rehearsal and knew how everything would take place. It went just as Johnson had told me it would a month earlier.

I have never known anyone who faced up to death with the same courage as Lyndon Johnson. He knew he was going to die from a heart attack; it was just a matter of when. He was in frequent pain and took a lot of pills to give him relief. Toward the end, he became almost pitiful. One day he backed up to the wall of a stone house on his land and told me that "they" had changed his medicine and he wasn't getting the pain relief he used to get. He said that they had even changed the color of the pills he was taking.

Johnson believed that the heart attack he had before his final, fatal one was brought on by his frustration at a speech he was supposed to make at a given function. He arrived on time, but the program had been delayed and he had to wait impatiently until it was his turn to speak. He said he was so frustrated by the continuing speeches of others that he was sure that had brought on the heart attack. Whether this was true or not, LBJ went to his grave believing it.

On more than one occasion, LBJ told me that he was hurt because he made the careers of so many people by giving them appointments in his administration and yet he seldom heard from anyone after he retired. He expected they would show him the courtesy of calling or writing him, or visiting him on the ranch. He was disappointed that they had forgotten him.

On the Saturday night before his death the following Monday, I called to tell him that I was going to Corpus Christi, Texas, on Monday to look after some of my oil and gas operations, and I wanted to spend the night at his ranch. LBJ told me all the reasons that I should come and spend Sunday with him as well as Monday. But I put him off, and on Monday, after I finished my business in South Texas, I called the Secret Service and told them that they should get the cows off of the runway by the time I arrived around 3 o'clock. They acknowledged the request and said the President was looking forward to my visit.

I landed on the ranch that afternoon as scheduled, but, unlike previous visits, there was no Lyndon Johnson sitting in the car waiting for me. We taxied up to the house and a Secret Service agent told me that I was not allowed to get out of the plane. He said that President Johnson was not there and that I could either wait in the plane or I could leave. I instinctively knew what had happened because we all had been expecting it for two years. After about an hour, LBJ's King Air plane came back and taxied up to the house and his secretary got out and came over to me crying. She said that the president had been taken to the hospital in San Antonio but was dead on arrival. She told me that the last thing he had said was, "I want to go get my nap so I'll be fresh when J. B. gets here."

CHAPTER 19

MEETING THE RICH AND FAMOUS

I have been fortunate to have met and become friends with many celebrities and notable people in my life, including presidents, vice presidents, senators, congressmen, prime ministers, Hollywood stars, and sports figures.

About 1970, I began looking for a real estate development opportunity for Fuqua Industries and found just what I wanted in Fort Lauderdale, Florida. Two brothers-in-law who operated as Haft and Gaines had just bought 1100 acres immediately west of the city. It was a beautiful piece of land in the country, and there were still cows grazing in the pastures. We made a stock-swap deal with Haft and Gaines that provided we would pay some shares of stock initially, as well as substantial additional shares over a period of years, based on the earnings.

Haft and Gaines designed a golf course development with two 18-hole courses, 25 tennis courts, and two clubhouses. The development, which we called Inverrary, was a success from the very beginning. We hired Jackie Gleason, whose *The Jackie Gleason Show* was a highly rated program on CBS at the time, and started a celebrity golf tournament that would be broadcast on CBS every spring. The Jackie Gleason Golf Tournament brought us good publicity for Inverrarry and helped us sell property in the development.

Gleason was not at all like the dummy he played on-screen. He had a limited education, but he was extremely well read and was one of the brightest people I have known. In addition to having a very satisfactory business relationship, he and I were good personal friends for years until he died. Gleason had a fear of heights and would not travel on an airplane. This was a plus for me because I imagined that if I had a similar celebrity without this fear, they might do a lot of traveling and not be available when I needed them. This was not likely to happen with Gleason, especially since the deal also involved our building a beautiful home for him at Inverrary on the golf course.

One of the early surprises Gleason pulled on me occurred during a press conference announcing the tournament. A reporter asked him about the amount of the purse for the winners. My heart almost stopped, for we had never discussed this with Gleason, or even among ourselves. I was afraid he might name some figure that would be totally inappropriate. Gleason responded that we would have the biggest purse any golf tournament had ever had. I got only more nervous as the press conference proceeded. The next reporter asked him if it was as much as $250,000. Gleason said, "It will be $250,000." This was a huge amount to pay for a beginning tournament, but we were stuck with it. As it worked out, the tournament was so popular and so valuable to our development sales, that that figure was not prohibitive.

CARL PATRICK

"We put on the Jackie Gleason golf tournament for seven or eight years and Inverarry was very successful. We were very fortunate. We had built about 400 units in a California style. Then we started building Florida style and they sold real fast. I was talking with Bert Haft and he said somebody wanted to come in and build the units for us. I asked him what they would pay us and he said $100,000 an acre. We had $20,000 an acre in the whole thing, including improvements, so I said, 'Bert, build two more buildings and sell the rest of it off.' At the end he was getting $135,000 an acre. When the bust came in Florida, there were 90,000 unsold condominums up along the beach and we didn't own one unsold one."

During this time, Jackie and his wife Beverly decided to get a divorce. He moved out of the house at Inverrary, but she would not leave. This became a real problem. We tried sending various representatives of the company to order her out of the house, including Gleason himself. Nothing seemed to frighten her, so I took it upon myself to deal with the situation. I went to see Beverly and told her in a very convincing way that she would have to move, or she would be forcibly removed. She finally took my words seriously and left the house after a few days.

Jackie had three wives over his lifetime. He later married a very nice lady, Marilyn, who had been one of the June Taylor dancers on his show. They lived together very happily until his death, and I was glad for him.

I gradually got Gleason weaned from his fear of flying by taking him places in my airplane. One year, we needed to get some fresh talent from Hollywood for the Pro-Am portion of the tournament. The plan was that I would take Gleason in my plane to Hollywood, where he would get some of his friends to agree to come to the tournament.

I knew that Jackie would have a problem with drinking along the way. Indeed, he started drinking almost immediately after we left the ground in Fort Lauderdale. As we neared Oklahoma City, where we were to stop for refueling, I began to realize that I would have a real problem if Gleason was not recognized as a celebrity when he landed. My luck was running well that day because he was recognized by several people when we entered the office of the refueling company.

He asked in a loud voice, "Where is the nearest bar?" We were told that the nearest bar would be in the passenger terminal on the other side of the field. This was about 10 o'clock in the morning and a man offered to drive us to the terminal so Gleason could have another drink. As we got closer to the cocktail lounge, I almost panicked again at the thought of how Gleason might behave in his inebriated state if he was not recognized by the people there. It would certainly be bad for his image.

We went into this bar and there was nobody there except the bartender, who did not recognize Gleason. Shortly thereafter, a lady came in who did know who he was and my fears disappeared. Soon he had several people hovering around him while he drank, and he was treated like the star he was. We went on to California and had no other incidents the rest of the trip. Jackie's drinking, however, was a real problem.

WINONA WARNER

"With Jackie Gleason, we had to have a bottle of Jack Daniels ready whenever he was in town. One time he came to the Masters at the last minute and we had to find a place for him to stay. Of course, all of the hotel rooms in Augusta had been booked up for months, so we found him a condo and bought linens and other furnishings. One thing he had to have every day was his carnation and his Jack Daniels."

Jackie had other personal problems, too, including a struggle with his weight. He would gain weight and then go on a binge to lose it by not eating for days on end. Dottie and I have been at his house for dinner when he sat at the table and ate nothing. Yet, regardless of his personal faults, Jackie Gleason was one of nicest and smartest people that I have ever had a relationship with.

When I first met Gerald Ford, he was the congressman from Grand Rapids, Michigan, where our trucking company Interstate Motor Freight Systems was located. I always contended that he was "my congressman," and we became good personal friends. When I started the Jackie Gleason tournament in Fort Lauderdale, Ford was invited to play in the Pro-Am section. When he became vice president, I thought for sure that he would not be able to participate, but he still did come and play. When he became president, I just figured that would be the end of the relationship, but it wasn't. Now, however, when he attended our golf tournaments, he was accompanied by a contingent of Secret Service agents and a number of sharpshooters who were stationed on the roofs of nearby buildings.

Until he became president, Gerald Ford was a frequent user of my airplane, a practice that once came in handy when an Internal Revenue agent arrived to review my airplane's log for a tax audit. The agent was flipping through the pages when he saw Gerald Ford's name appear several times. He immediately shut the logbook, turned to one of my associates and said, "I don't want to see this anymore." And that was the end of that tax audit.

In return for our hospitality with the Inverrary tournament, Dottie and I and the Gleasons were invited to President Ford's tournament in Vail, Colorado, several times. When the Fords had a big party for their 35th wedding anniversary in Palm Springs, California, Dottie and I were apparently the only two guests invited from the East. Needless to say, we have enjoyed our friendship with the Fords very much.

We have known many other interesting people, but a special treat was getting to meet the Dalai Lama. My son Rex had visited him in India once with a National Geographic photographer and, as he was leaving, Rex asked the Dalai Lama to let us return the hospitality the next time he came to the U.S. Sure enough, Rex got a call one day in 1995 saying the Dalai Lama would be coming to Atlanta to speak at Emory University. Dottie and I hosted a reception for this fascinating man at our home with about 50 other couples. He turned out to be a rather jolly fellow who seemed to enjoy every moment greeting people and having his picture taken in our very appropriate Oriental garden.

Dottie and I joined Lady Bird Johnson in Charleston in 1964
aboard the "Lady Bird Express."

LBJ and I posed with the famous deer I finally caught on his ranch.

Jackie Gleason, President Gerald Ford, and I exchanged greetings at a party for Gleason at the Diplomat Hotel in Florida in 1977.

Former President Jimmy Carter and I recall our days as members of the Georgia State Senate at a political reunion.

Dottie and I visited with President and Mrs. Ford at the World Forum in Beaver Creek, Colorado, in June 1990.

The former president and I entertained Mikhail Gorbachev when
he visited Atlanta in 1992.

Rex, Dottie, and I posed for the camera in 2000.

PART
VI

GIVING
SOMETHING BACK

CHAPTER 20

TAKING CAPITALISM
TO THE RUSSIANS

In the late 1980s as I approached my 70th birthday, I began to think about the ways I could spend my time after retirement that would be interesting and make a worthwhile contribution to society. I don't know why I thought I needed to retire and, in retrospect, I would have been much better off if I had stayed in business. As it happened, however, I was able to accomplish something that gave me great satisfaction and helped contribute to international understanding.

At the time, I had become interested in the Soviet Union as an economic power and trading partner for our country, and I had a gut feeling that the USSR was about to break up. I had read a lot of Mikhail Gorbachev's speeches, and I noticed that he said over and over that he didn't need Western money or Western loans, he just needed Western know-how to implement perestroika. Tremendous resources were being spent on the Cold War at the time, and it occurred to me that I might be able to furnish some of this know-how Gorbachev said he needed and thereby help to speed up the breakup of the Soviet Union.

In any society or industry you can pick out a small number of people who can make a big difference. I thought that if I could take the top managers of the Russian companies — they called them directors, we call them chief executive officers — and get those people to understand the free market system, we could create widespread changes in Russia. I decided the way to accomplish this was to bring the top managers of a number of Russian businesses to the U.S. to study our system.

I gave The Fuqua School of Business $4 million to facilitate my program and we set a goal of bringing over 300 general manager types ranging in age from 35 to 50 over a number of years. We didn't want middle managers or anybody running a small business; we wanted people who could make decisions. I didn't know a thing in the world about how to do this, but I knew that if I could get access to the top people in the Russian government, I could make it work. I decided not to go to our State Department for assistance, but I did advise them about the project.

My next step was contacting Armand Hammer, a wealthy and influential businessman who was on good terms with the Russians. He told me that what I wanted to do was of such importance that I ought to go see Gorbachev directly. However, if I wanted to get it done much faster, I should go to the number-three man in the government, an economist who would understand my plan. If I could get his cooperation, Hammer said, everything else would fall into place.

Well, with the help of the American ambassador, I set up a meeting with Leonid Abalkin, Russia's deputy prime minister, and other officials. We were treated like royalty. Tom Keller, dean of The Fuqua School of Business, the U.S. ambassador, and I were taken to the Kremlin in a limousine that sped through the streets of Moscow with an escort front and back going 50 miles an hour. It was exciting, to say the least.

I took an interpreter with me and proceeded to tell the Soviet officials about The Fuqua School of Business and what my plan entailed. I was getting into my story pretty good when one of the fellows I had come to see, Abel G. Aganbegyan, interrupted me and said, "Mr. Fuqua, I know all about The Fuqua School of Business. I've been to your school." It turned out that two years earlier he had been to the school as an economist. After that, we got along well. Mr. Aganbegyan, who was the head of the Academy of National Economy of the USSR Council of Ministers and one of the most powerful men in the Soviet Union, became our USSR partner.

The first agreement was drawn up and typed in Russian and when I asked my interpreter to go over it, he said he found one thing that they had set up where everything was to their advantage. Overall, however, they cooperated and we reached agreement on how the program would be implemented.

We needed someone to run the program who could

speak Russian fluently and who understood the Russian way of doing business. We ran an ad in the Paris *Herald Tribune* and had the good fortune of receiving an application from Jeff Smith, who had been a business representative for General Electric in the Eastern European countries for several years. In addition, Smith was married to a Russian woman who had been a professional translator. Once we got Smith on board, we made good progress toward getting our program activated.

The first class of Russians arrived at The Fuqua School of Business in Durham, North Carolina, in 1990. We had to have a partner on the Russian end to help us select the students who would attend. The Russians advertised for applicants and then selected fifty from the hundreds of applications they received. We then selected the top thirty through conducting interviews in the candidates' workplaces or homes. We wanted to be sure we got the best prospects, people who would get the maximum out of the training course. Since the Soviet Union was still in place, we tried to select businessmen from all the separate republics. They arrived in Washington on Aeroflot and were transported to Durham by bus after a tour of our nation's capital.

In the program, we gave them intense instruction: three weeks of 10-hour days on how the free market system operates, how profits are made, and how costs are figured. One of the problems with the system the Soviets used was that they didn't know how to do costing. If you don't know what something costs, you can't put a price on it. Some of them guessed right and made big profits while others made no profits. Under the Communist system, it didn't seem to make much difference.

I went over there in February 1989 and the Soviet Union fell apart in 1991. I would like to think that I had something to do with the breakup and the tearing down of the Berlin Wall. The first hint I got that the Soviet Union was about to break up came from some events in Hungary. Hungary hated the Russians because the Russians had come in there with tanks during an uprising in 1956 and killed a bunch of Hungarian civilians. I saw evidence of the cracks in the Soviet Union when I went to Budapest in 1989 and 1990 at the request of the American ambassador. Sure enough, the first break came in Hungary after the government started allowing the people to go across the border into East Germany. I was visiting the ambassador in Budapest in 1991 when I saw the Hungarians removing the red stars from the government buildings as they celebrated their freedom.

The whole Soviet Union collapsed as one country after another split off. The conventional wisdom was that Gorbachev had freed these people because he was such a kind, gentle person, but in reality he had told the leaders of these countries that they would have to deal with any internal problems on their own with no help from Moscow. When that word got out, the people who were opposed to the Soviet government began to come alive.

From an economic standpoint, Russia was almost broke and they had 400,000 troops in Hungary alone. They had a huge military force scattered all through these

Eastern European countries that were satellites of the Soviet Union. Gorbachev was the first educated head of that country, and he realized he had to do something. He could not afford to keep paying for the large army, and he had to reduce the budget. When he slashed the military budget, the Soviet Union fell apart and he signed an agreement to let the soldiers all go. Tom Johnson, the president of CNN, was there when the agreement was finalized in 1991, and he had to loan Gorbachev a pen with which to sign it. Tom still carries the pen.

When we brought the Soviet business leaders here in 1990, we matched them up with companies that were similar to their specialties. If they were in the consumer products business, for example, we'd put them with Coca-Cola or some company that was as close as possible to their business.

At the time we started our program, the Soviet economy was in awful shape. There wasn't anything in the stores, and people had to stand in line to buy what bread and milk was left. Unlike other countries such as Japan, where consumer spending was high, the Russians didn't buy much, because there wasn't much available. They had nothing to spend their money on, so their savings rate was extremely high.

For 70 years in the Soviet Union, every factory was managed by the government. They had quotas, and the country's economy was totally mismanaged. They never learned to convert to capitalism. Gorbachev's idea was that they were all going to a capitalist system but they would still keep some of the government control. They planned to take the money that was going to the military and put it to use in civilian production making consumer products.

In Moscow and the main cities now, they have everything for sale on the shelves that we have in this country. Before the breakup, they made automobiles but people couldn't afford to buy them and they were of very poor quality because there was no competition. There are more foreign automobiles on the street there now, and gradually the country is making progress.

The U.S. could have done more to help the Soviet Union, and it is my opinion that the CIA will be indicted by historians for their actions. They were telling our government how much power the Soviet Union had, but their tanks and equipment were of such poor quality that they never would have lasted if actually put to the test.

I did several interviews on Russian TV and had a high profile over there. I also visited the homes of poor people as well as the residences of the richest people in Russia. I went to homes where three or four families lived in three or four rooms with one kitchen and one bathroom. One night I went to dinner with a fellow who had been through our business school and who obviously was on his way up. He lived with his wife, small son, and grandfather. His wife spoke a little English, and we had a delightful conversation. During one discussion, someone brought up a question about one of the American presidents, and the grandfather knew more about American history than I did. They had sent him to Siberia for several years, and while he was there he had read all the books available about the U.S. presidents. He told me many things I didn't know.

The Russian exchange program with The Fuqua School of Business proved to be very successful. Some of the people who went through the program are millionaires now, while others fell into the old groove and didn't accomplish much. I started the program with $4 million and I thought if I got a dozen industry leaders, my money would be well spent. Actually, I got several dozen. You go to Russia today and you will find that the telecommunications industry is largely controlled by people who were in my program.

I still hear from some of the people who appreciate so much what I did for them. They have an alumni group that meets frequently, and I have been entertained by them on my trips to Russia. Indeed, this program has been the most satisfactory philanthropy I have ever done.

CHAPTER 21

SUPPORTING EDUCATION

Capitalism, or the free enterprise system, is often said to produce an unequal distribution of wealth. Frankly, I have been one
of the very fortunate. While the wealthy are seldom applauded
in this country, without the donations of some very generous
people we would be short on educational institutions, churches, museums, hospitals, and many other things that enrich and
distinguish our society from those of socialist countries.

Fame can disappear like the morning fog. Popularity is
often an accident. Riches can vanish in a day. Yet for over
three centuries, there have been outstanding individuals in
this country who have shared their wealth in a manner that
contributed to society well beyond their lifetimes. That is one
of my aims.

It was the wealth of prosperous pioneer landowner John

Harvard that made possible Harvard University. It was the railroad fortune of Leland Stanford that created Stanford University. Tennessee is the home of Vanderbilt, another great institution created by a railroad fortune. Duke University, in which I have a special interest, came into being by the Duke family's fortune from tobacco and electrical power, and of course The Fuqua School of Business came from my own philanthropy. No one can deny how sharing has helped us become the best-equipped society on earth.

The rich make their money from their money; they make their mark by what they give and what they share. In the early 1980s I was flattered to be listed as one of Forbes' 400 Richest Americans. While my family's net worth is into nine figures today, I no longer belong in that category. But I am so very grateful for my wealth, and I have tried to share it in a manner that reaches many who are not so fortunate.

I determine my philanthropy primarily through my personal account. However, I also have The J. B. Fuqua Foundation, which I started in 1972 with a modest base. The foundation has an advantage in that funds put into it are deductible for tax purposes at the time they are contributed to the foundation and its earnings are tax free. To illustrate the benefits of compound interest where the interest is reinvested, I have put a total of $23 million into this foundation, I have paid out $22 million to various charities, and I still have a balance in the foundation of about $30 million.

I also have a trust from which I pay philanthropic commitments, but most of my larger charitable grants are made out of my personal account. The recipient has no way of knowing what account the money comes from; it is simply an accounting procedure that has certain benefits to me.

I hope to give away much of my fortune before I die, but in my will I have provided for additional funds for some of the beneficiaries of my philanthropy. Other organizations will become beneficiaries of my estate as well. I am sometimes asked what I have gotten from my giving of so much. The most positive thing I can say to emphasize the good feeling of giving is that the more I give, the more I have.

One of the most important ways I have found to give is through education. One night I went to my office at WJBF Television in Augusta and found a young black man cleaning the floor. When I asked him if he would take my car and go to our post office box to get the mail, he was somewhat embarrassed and said he couldn't do that because he couldn't drive.

I knew nothing about him, but I immediately visualized what a bleak future it would be for a man who had no ability to make any kind of living other than by what he was doing. As we talked, the young man, Edet Okepebeke, explained that he was a student from Nigeria at Paine College in Augusta, but that he was going to have to drop out because both of his parents had been killed in a civil war and he could no longer earn enough income to pay for college. His story touched me so deeply that I decided to pay his way through Paine College.

WINONA WARNER

"Mr. Fuqua did a lot of things quietly that didn't get public attention. Not only did he pay for Edet Okepebeke's education, he gave him a job at the television station while he was going to school. This young man kept in contact with me for years and often told me how grateful he was to Mr. Fuqua."

Edet was a very intelligent young man, and the last I heard he was making a good living as a pharmacist. He was the first of many students that I was able to help.

THE FUQUA SCHOOL OF BUSINESS

I have always been grateful to Duke University for the library books I was able to borrow by mail when growing up on the farm in Virginia, so when Duke President Terry Sanford mentioned that the university needed a business school, I decided to give them $10 million to start it. Sanford, a former governor of North Carolina, was a director of Fuqua Industries at the time and we had become close personal friends.

Terry Sanford was a great salesman. I succumbed to his appeals for the need for Duke to have a world-class business school and that it would be only appropriate for it to be named The Fuqua School of Business. Being egotistical, that of course appealed to me, but my principal motivation was the feeling that my generation of business leaders did not make as effective use of natural and human resources as they might have, had they had more education. I made the commitment of $10 million one night in a telephone call from my airplane and Sanford subsequently referred to his having gotten "a call from on high" that enabled Duke to have The Fuqua School of Business.

Over the years, I have given more than $37 million to The Fuqua School of Business, which is by far the largest beneficiary of my philanthropy. Next to the Duke family's own contributions, this is more than anyone has given to Duke University.

I have seen so many instances in which a well-meaning individual will donate a large amount of money for a project and then dismiss it from his or her mind. In my case, I have tried to assist in the development of The Fuqua School of Business through my contacts and my business experience. The Fuqua School of Business currently ranks Number 5 in the *Business Week* survey of business schools and also ranks close to the top in other surveys. I am very proud of such recognition. My son, Rex, is on the Board of Trustees of Duke University, I am a Trustee Emeritus, and both of us are on the Board of Visitors of The Fuqua School of Business.

PRINCE EDWARD ACADEMY

It is usually gratifying when one can do something for his or her hometown, but donors need to be careful about certain kinds of philanthropic enterprises that require perpetual funding with no matching contributions and little appreciation from the beneficiaries.

I mention this because of a situation that I became involved in in my home county. In 1959, the leaders of Prince Edward County, Virginia, were so upset by the federal court's orders for the integration of public schools that they attempted to solve their problem by simply shutting down the schools so that no black would sit in the same classroom with a white child. They went around the community passing the hat for contributions to develop a private school called Prince Edward Academy in Farmville. They set this up so that white children could get an education, but the black children got no education whatever. This went on for several years until the federal court required the county to provide schools for the blacks. The public schools thus became primarily for the black children and Prince Edward Academy was for the whites.

Support for the Prince Edward Academy came from people all over the country who were far-right segregationists. They had never been to Farmville, but they were so convinced that the world would come to an end if blacks and whites were in the same classroom that they sent donations totaling millions of dollars. I never gave a penny to the Prince Edward Academy during this time.

However, in 1991, I got a desperate telephone call from Robert Taylor, with whom I had grown up. Taylor, who was a principal leader in the "segregation at any cost" movement in Prince Edward County, told me that the school had a large debt with the Sovran Bank, which was a part of Citizens & Southern Bank headquartered in Atlanta. The bank was foreclosing and they would lose the school entirely if they did not get some kind of relief. I knew that the management of the C&S Bank in Atlanta would be surprised to learn they were about to get into the private school business, so I talked to Bennett Brown, who was then CEO of C&S, and told him what his bank was in the process of doing. He was amazed that the bank had gotten itself into this situation and gratefully accepted my offer to pay off the debt of $1 million.

While the federal courts had forced Prince Edward Academy to open its doors to blacks some years earlier, there were only three black children out of 600 students. It should be said in fairness that the major cause of this was that blacks in the area did not have the money to send their children to private school, even though the tuition was relatively low.

I made a proposition that I would pay off the debt provided the school conduct a fund-raising drive of $1 million to match my million. This would give them some operating capital for another year. I also stipulated that part of these funds were to be used as scholarships for minority students. Having gotten into the situation at Prince Edward Academy, I decided to go ahead and make it a model school for rural areas.

I air-conditioned the present school, built additional buildings, and modernized the school in every respect, including putting in a computer for every two students.

The name was changed to The Fuqua School, and I was very proud of myself for what I was doing for my hometown community. The Fuqua School is now a model rural independent school that compares well with any private preparatory school in the country. In addition to having Ruth Murphy as a top administrator, Fuqua School has an excellent faculty and a modern 60-acre campus. It is well supported by technology and is operated by a local board of directors. Unfortunately, Fuqua School is a long way from being self-supporting. There are no other large benefactors and it costs me about $400,000 a year to underwrite the school's losses, but I hope this deficit will decline in the future.

PACE ACADEMY

Often institutions seeking a charitable grant need some help in structuring the best and most efficient use of the money they seek. An example of this was a solicitation from Pace Academy, a private school in Atlanta, for $1 million to enhance its debating activities. The headmaster had heard of my interest in debating when I was in high school, and he very creatively sought me out to underwrite his expansion idea.

I analyzed the proposal and made a counterproposal that I thought better suited their needs. I suggested that $1 million was not enough to accomplish what they wanted and that I would give them $1.2 million. This larger amount was to be in the form of a Chair of Public Speaking and Debate at Pace Academy, and it would provide for a payment from the trust of 10 percent annually. They had planned to use 6 percent of the $1 million they solicited, or $60,000 a year. My plan immediately gave them $72,000 a year, which enabled them to have an entirely different level of operation of their debating program. It would seem that this would extinguish the whole fund in less than 10 years, but Pace has been getting more than 10 percent return on its endowment investments, and I feel that it could probably operate in perpetuity based on a 10 percent payout. In any event, by giving them $1.2 million, I gave them twice as much income as they had anticipated in their original proposal. I have often made similar counterproposals for philanthropic projects in which I have become interested.

JUNIOR ACHIEVEMENT INTERNATIONAL

My most recent large philanthropic project has just been completed after more than two years of efforts. I made a proposal to Junior Achievement International that I would give them $4 million to expand its programs in the more than 100 countries in which it now operates. Junior Achievement International, the global arm of Junior Achievement, teaches economics, free enterprise, and entrepreneurship to students and provides wonderful opportunities for young people in different countries to work together. It makes better use of its money than any nonprofit I am familiar with, and reaches over a million students per year at a surprisingly low cost per student.

When considering a gift of this size, I'm careful about doing due diligence on the particular operation. For example, I wanted to make sure this gift could be used as a springboard to attract other significant donors necessary to fund further expansion. I found out, though, that Junior

Achievement International was seriously restricted in its fund-raising efforts. I learned that they needed permission from the national and local Junior Achievements to call on, for example, Coca-Cola — even though Coke has more interests in more countries than any other American company. This prevented Junior Achievement International from raising the kind of funds needed to seriously beef up its operation. The situation has now hopefully been corrected so the groups can work more cohesively, but it took a couple of years to iron out. I also sent my foundation's program director, Anne Sterchi, to Russia, the Czech Republic, and Ireland to get a firsthand view of how some of the international offices operate.

I am giving Junior Achievement International $800,000 a year for the next five years, which is nearly a 50 percent increase in its operating budget. This should enable them to make significant enhancements in their operations and infrastructure to support substantial growth targets.

COLLEGE FUNDS

Some of my best smaller philanthropies are the $5,000 awards that I give to teachers from a variety of colleges and universities located outside Georgia who have been selected for recognition by former students three to five years after the students have graduated. A CPA firm mails ballots in the spring to all former students who fit the formula asking for nominations of one or two faculty members who have been the most valuable professor he or she had in college.

The $5,000 award is enough to get the attention of all college faculty and, since this is a consumer survey, it measures the quality of the product after it has been used. It is a real incentive for college faculty members, and it is one of the most satisfying things I do for colleges and universities. Some teachers oppose the program, however, and say the survey should ask the faculty to evaluate each other. That would defeat the purpose of this project, just as an evaluation carried out while the students are still in school would be no more than a popularity contest.

SCHOLARSHIPS AND ENDOWMENTS

Endowed professorships, or chairs as they are called, make a nice permanent gift that can be given to honor someone. I gave The Fuqua School of Business a $2.3 million chair of international management in the name of my son Rex in 1997. Dottie gave the University of Georgia a $2.5 million chair for the business school in Rex's name, and she also gave $2.5 million for music scholarships to Presbyterian College in Clinton, South Carolina.

CHAPTER 22

ENHANCING THE COMMUNITY

I have given away over $100 million in my lifetime, and I have always looked for philanthropic causes that I thought were worthy. For example, when I was living in Augusta in the late 1950s and early 1960s, there were city-funded recreation facilities for whites but nothing for blacks. After much pressure from black voters, the City Council finally approved a Negro Recreation Department to provide blacks with some degree of organized sports and recreation. However, the city only provided a place for the activities to take place and repeatedly failed to authorize any significant funds.

This concerned me so much that I began providing baseballs, footballs, basketballs, and other types of recreation and sporting equipment at my own expense. The city did pay a very modest sum to W. T. Johnson to be the director of the Negro

Recreation Department, but in reality I was W. T.'s biggest budget source. Among other things, I paid his expenses to travel to other cities to see what was being done in the area of recreation for blacks.

I was ashamed of the Augusta community for this racist attitude. I sometimes felt I was the only one who thought that blacks should have the same benefits from the city budget as whites. What I did amounted to only a small gesture at the time, but I thought it was important to be able to provide something that would improve my local community. Dottie and I have always tried in the years since to give to projects in our adopted hometown of Atlanta that have improved cultural resources and offered opportunities for everyone.

ATLANTA BOTANICAL GARDEN

The Atlanta Botanical Garden is really Dottie's project. In November 1989, the Atlanta Botanical Garden opened the Dorothy Chapman Fuqua Conservatory, which I often refer to as my $5.5 million glass house. This is a state-of-the-art building with a staff whose mission is to develop and maintain plant collections, especially rare, threatened, and unusual varieties. Dottie has been interested in flowers and plants ever since she helped her grandmother in her English-style cottage garden in Davisboro during the Depression.

DOTTIE FUQUA

"I was on the board of the Botanical Garden and when I'd come in from a meeting J. B. would ask what we had discussed. I said we're never going to be a first-class garden until we have a conservatory. He said, 'Well, how much would it cost?' I said I didn't know but I would find out. I called the director, Ann Crammond, the next day and asked her. She said, 'Oh, at least a million dollars. That's just out of the question.' J. B. and I went to dinner a few nights later and I told him I found out the conservatory would cost a million dollars. He didn't say a word and two weeks later he came in and said, 'Well, I put $2 million in the bank for your project.' I nearly fell over."

When we began considering the project, the Botanical Garden existed more in name than fact because it did not have a conservatory. Dottie and I and the director Ann Crammond visited conservatories in a number of cities and foreign countries to get some ideas before we announced the gift. We advanced the Botanical Garden funds as needed for the construction of the conservatory. Our initial gift ended up being $5.5 million. We have since made other donations to the Atlanta Botanical Garden, including a gift of $3 million in 1997 for the Orchid House addition to the conservatory, which is now being built. Our total contribution to the Atlanta Botanical Garden is nearly $10 million.

The Atlanta Botanical Garden has more than 10,000 members, and the Conservatory and the Orchid House are the principal attractions. I often think that if we had not developed these facilities, the Botanical Garden would be a minor attraction compared to what it is today. There are so many instances in which the funds of one person or one family alone have supported some very important nonprofit recreational or cultural project.

PIEDMONT HOSPITAL

Dottie and I are deeply involved with the Fuqua Heart Center at Piedmont Hospital. When we first moved to Atlanta from Augusta, we used Emory Hospital to take care of our health needs, but as we got older we realized that it would be nice to have a first-class heart center closer to our home, in one of north Atlanta's older neighborhoods. The drive to Emory takes about 30 minutes, while the distance from our home to Piedmont Hospital is only four miles. If either of us had a heart attack in the middle of the night, our survival rate would largely be related to how long it took to get proper medical attention. If we could establish a top-notch heart facility at Piedmont, we thought, who knows how many older Atlantans like us would benefit from it?

As our 50th wedding anniversary approached in 1995, we offered to make a grant to Piedmont that would enable the hospital to develop the best heart center facility in Atlanta. We gave an initial $3 million grant on our anniversary and since then we have given a total of $7.5 million. We are extremely proud of the Fuqua Heart Center, and we are particularly touched by the splendid morale of the professional staff, the administrators, and the support people. My personal cardiologist, Dr. Mark Silverman, has taken wonderful care of me and has been a trusted friend. Perhaps I have a special feeling for this project because in 1999 I had a five-way bypass at the Fuqua Heart Center and Dottie has had a pacemaker operation performed there.

My doctor at Piedmont, Dr. Marshall Levine, is an exceptional physician. He will come to my home if necessary and, on those occasions when he is going out of town, he leaves his telephone number where he can be reached. He has always urged me to call him anywhere or anytime if I have a physical problem. It has been a pleasure to help Piedmont Hospital develop a world-class heart facility, and the favor has been repaid to us by the generosity of the wonderful doctors we've seen there.

In addition to making a grant to Piedmont Hospital for the Fuqua Heart Center, I have provided for the staff's special needs over the years. As an example, in June 2001 I committed to buy them a new type of imaging machine that will cost more than $1 million.

I have been generous to Piedmont for personal as well as philanthropic reasons. My health has always been a concern to me, and I have been hospitalized many times for everything from tuberculosis to gallbladder removal to

five-way heart bypass surgery. I never was a big, strong ath-
letic type, perhaps because I never participated in sports,
but I would say that I have average health for a man 83
years old. Having said that, I can assure you that 83 isn't the
same as 63.

ATLANTA UNION MISSION

When I had my office in the Georgia Pacific building, I
often noticed a line forming in the early evening across the
street on Ellis Street in front of the Atlanta Union Mission.
The men in line were coming to get an evening meal, and it
frequently occurred to me that, but for the luck of the draw,
I could be one of those people in that line. While I had been
making modest gifts to the Atlanta Union Mission for several years, I determined that I should do more. In the past
few years, I have given cumulative gifts of $2.5 million to
the Atlanta Union Mission and will give a significant
amount to a capital fund drive that the Union Mission will
be going into in 2002.

There are many good organizations serving poor people,
but none is any more worthy than the Atlanta Union Mission.
In 1996 I contributed $1 million to convert a facility built to
house press representatives for the 1996 Olympics into a
transitional residence hall for men. It is called Fuqua Hall and
is located on Techwood Drive downtown. Fuqua Hall offers
an 18-month program to help alcoholics and drug addicts
and others who are down on their luck get back on their feet
and into an independent and self-sufficient lifestyle. Fuqua

Hall is a temporary home to 90 men and it feeds about 400 men every night who otherwise would have no place to get a warm meal. This is the kind of charity that I can see and feel, and I get more pleasure from it than I do giving to something like the Red Cross and other big national organizations.

THE ELDERLY

I have a special interest in old people, perhaps because I am now old myself. So many elderly who appear to have lost an interest in things are assumed to be merely old, when in fact they are really very depressed. Atlanta's principal geriatric hospital is Wesley Woods, which specializes in treating mental illness. Between Wesley Woods and the George West Mental Health Foundation, which Dottie is interested in, we have invested over $4 million in mental health programs in just the last few years. Wesley Woods has the Fuqua Center for Late-Life Depression that seeks out older people and treats them for depression. They do some really remarkable work. I have an elderly friend who had one episode of depression and he could not recognize me or other friends or even his children. After a week's treatment, he has totally recovered and has no recurrence of this frightening experience.

CHAPTER 23

SPECIAL GIFTS
FOR WORTHY CAUSES

Once you become a philanthropist, everywhere you turn, you find people in need. Somewhere you have to draw the line and decide to pursue organizations that mean something to you personally. But sometimes a very special opportunity comes along to help out in a very unique way, and I enjoy doing so when I'm able.

AN OLYMPIC GIFT

In the spring of 1996 when Atlanta was feverishly preparing for the opening of the summer Olympics, there was publicity every day in the newspapers about the venues where the various events would be held. One morning I was impressed by a story in the *Atlanta Constitution* about the fact that spectators would have to take public transportation to the venues instead of being allowed to drive their cars. This meant there would be a lot of waiting in the hot July climate before and after an event. It occurred to me that millions of visitors to Atlanta would not have access to water or something to drink and they would not have adequate sanitary facilities at the venues.

I called Billy Payne, who was the president of the Atlanta Committee for the Olympic Games, and his associate, A. D. Frazier, and asked them if they planned to do anything about this situation. Frazier said they had not been able to budget the cost of providing water or sanitary facilities at the many venues where the Games would take place. I could not believe that we were going to put on a successful Olympics unless we could provide adequate facilities for spectators to get a drink of water and answer the call of nature. Frazier said this was just something that regrettably would be missing from the Atlanta Olympics. They estimated that the cost of providing a minimum of water and sanitary facilities would be about $2 million. I told them that I could not willingly let that amount of money stand in the way of the comfort of our millions of guests, and that I would personally give the Olympics Committee $1.5 million to provide portable toilets and water containers for those waiting in the hot sun at the various venues.

Both Billy Payne and A. D. Frazier were amazed that an individual who had not been asked to contribute anything toward the operation of the Olympics would make such a proposal. I provided money for the renting of portable toilets and water barrels and it became obvious to any observer during the Games that to deny the public these facilities would have been very poor hospitality on the part of the city. There was considerable publicity in connection with this gift. One cartoon that I particularly remember showed me as an Olympic runner with a streaming roll of toilet paper. This cartoon resulted in a lot of kidding, all of which I took in good spirits. I was delighted that Atlanta got a huge amount of worldwide publicity because of the Olympics, and I was pleased to be able to make our visitors a little more comfortable.

THE CRYSTAL CATHEDRAL

One of the more unusual projects I have created or helped develop is the Fuqua International School of Christian Communication at Dr. Robert Schuller's Crystal Cathedral in California. I got to know Schuller through our membership in the Horatio Alger Association, and we became good friends. I like Schuller because his sermons are uplifting lectures and he never tries to convert his listeners. He is always upbeat and never uses words like *hell, sin, damnation, devil,* or other scary terms.

One time Schuller was at our home in Atlanta when we got into a discussion of the fact that many preachers are brilliant academically, but they do a very poor job of delivering their message. In other words, they need training in public speaking. This is especially true in many small churches in rural communities, more so than in cities where preachers are paid a larger salary. I told Schuller that if he would take a floor in his building adjacent to the Crystal Cathedral and convert it into a school for preachers, I would give him $2 million to cover the cost of renovation and equipment.

For several years now, Schuller has been running the Fuqua International School of Christian Communication as a series of one-week intensive training programs in effective public speaking, using some of the best dramatic teaching talent available in Hollywood. We get preachers from small country churches and big city churches, from the largest Episcopalian congregations to the small churches of minor denominations. A video is made of the student's sermon when he enters the course, and another video is produced when he has finished. I get letters from preachers all over the world expressing their appreciation and telling us how much the courses in dramatic training have done for them and their churches. I am glad to be able to help a fine man like Bob Schuller who teaches and acts lovingly and is a positive thinker. This is the kind of philanthropy that gives me a real sense of satisfaction.

THE LIBRARY OF CONGRESS

One would think that giving away money would be easy, but that is not always the case. Some years ago I tried without success to give $1 million to the Library of Congress. They have hundreds of thousands of items on their Web site and they're adding more all the time. It is the greatest source of man's knowledge anywhere in the world. People who are librarians or archivists are good at collecting information, but they frequently aren't good at distributing it. The Library of Congress is a great national resource that, until the development of the Internet, was good only for the people who could go to Washington and go into the various buildings and get books to do their research. With the development of the Internet, everything worthwhile will be available anywhere in the world for those who have a computer connection.

When I went to the little country high school in Virginia, they had a little library about 10 x 12 feet with mostly books of fiction. If I had had the resources of the Library of Congress available to me when I was in high school, I would not have gone through the motions of borrowing books from the Duke University library. I would have gotten a much better education because I would have read lots more and learned more.

Now, if you have a computer and the Internet, you can go to the Web site for the Library of Congress and you have the ability to access vast stores of information that have been collected since the time of Thomas Jefferson.

I thought that the use of the Library of Congress by schools all over the country would enable smaller schools in rural areas to have access to as fine a library as any big city institution. I offered the Library of Congress $1 million to set up a program to train teachers how to use the Library of Congress. They were enthusiastic about it initially, but as we went along it was clear that the way they wanted to do it didn't fit in with my plans. Since I was going to pay for it, I thought we should do it in the most efficient way to train teachers.

They wanted to have a program whereby teachers would come to Washington for tutoring. It was obvious to me that the expense of hauling teachers to Washington when it could be done in a simpler manner was ridiculous. I made tentative arrangements for the University of Georgia to run the whole program. It was practical and it was in my budget. The only problem was, it was not part of the federal government and the people at the Library of Congress thought they would not have sufficient control of the program. If I had gone forward with this project, I would have gotten mixed up with having to give each of the 50 states equal benefits from the program. We would have had to make the program fit into the Library of Congress's idea of racial equality and several other things I soon learned I would encounter in trying to give $1 million to the library. I finally abandoned the idea. And I regret that many of those teachers probably still don't know how to make use of all the Library of Congress has to offer.

SMALL GIFTS THAT MATTER

Even very small projects can make a big difference. In Atlanta, there is a lady named Jennifer Bruner who trains dogs to do all kinds of tasks that make life much easier for people with certain kinds of disabilities. I am one of the largest benefactors of Bruner's organization, Canine Assistants, and it is something that is very, very satisfactory to me.

In the late '70s, I gave a number of carillon bells to churches in the areas where Dottie had grown up and in my home county in Virginia. These are electronic bells that are set to ring and play hymns twice a day. It is rewarding to know that these bells bring joy to many people day in and day out.

A few years ago, I began giving computers to older people who have never had one and who thought they were too complicated to use. I gave one to Emma Berry, who is a 70-year-old cousin living in Fort Lauderdale, and it has literally changed her life. She lives alone and, having gotten a computer, she has made many friends on the Internet whom she communicates with regularly. I also gave computers to my friends Charles West and Bob Redfearn, who found that they are wonderful tools that can really change one's lifestyle.

I got particular pleasure from giving a computer to Winona Warner, who was my secretary for 20 years and who worked for me for a longer period of time. She is about 80 years old now and, like Emma Berry, she has in many ways made a new life for herself through the computer.

WINONA WARNER

"Mr. Fuqua called me one day and said, 'Would you use a computer if you had one?' I said, 'Well, I guess I would.' He said, 'Well, I want you to get one. Get a pen and write this down.' He gave me the specifications of the computer I would get, then he said to go pick out the kind I wanted, pay for it, send him the receipt, and he would mail me a check for it. I knew nothing about computers, but I went and bought one. I have thoroughly enjoyed mine and in fact, I'm addicted to it."

Philanthropy in all its many forms has given me great personal satisfaction. Giving to these people and organizations has enriched my life as much as I hope my contributions have enriched theirs.

J.B. FUQUA CONTRIBUTIONS OF $1 MILLION OR MORE

American Enterprise Institute
Atlanta Botanical Garden
Atlanta Committee for the Olympic Games
Atlanta Union Mission
Crystal Cathedral
Duke University—The Fuqua School of Business
Fuqua School
Hampden-Sydney College
House Ear Institute
Junior Achievement International
Lovett School
Pace Academy
Piedmont Hospital—Fuqua Heart Center
Presbyterian College
Salvation Army
Shepherd Center
Trinity School
United Way
University of Georgia—Terry College of Business
Wesley Woods/Emory—Fuqua Center for Late-Life Depression
George West Mental Health Foundation/Skyland Trail

PART
VII

A FEW REFLECTIONS

CHAPTER 24

MY PERSONAL STRUGGLES

Just because I have lived the classic American success story does not mean my life has been free from trials. I overcame a very unhappy childhood to find personal and professional rewards in the business world. But there have been some real low points in my life as well.

The greatest tragedy of my life was the death of my second son, Alan, who was killed in a plane crash when he was an 18-year-old student at the University of Georgia. When threatened with being drafted for the Vietnam war, both Rex and Alan enlisted in the Georgia Air National Guard so they could continue college. The National Guard was a major commitment. Enlistees were required to sign up for six years of service, which included six months of basic training, two weeks of training every summer, and one weekend of duty each month. But unless the Air National Guard was called to active duty, Rex and Alan would thankfully stay out of that unpopular war.

Every parent old enough to have had a son of draft age during the Vietnam War knows that feeling of yearning for the safety of their child. They remember that the lead story on the network evening news every night was the rising body count, and it was accompanied by horrifying pictures of body bags. And all of this was happening because we were "fighting communism" in some place we couldn't even locate on a map.

Alan missed a National Guard weekend duty schedule in Macon, Georgia, in 1970, and traveled with two college buddies to Jacksonville to a makeup duty there instead. They were returning from Jacksonville to Athens in a single-engine plane piloted by the father of one of Alan's friends on board. The air traffic controller in Macon failed to warn the pilot of a severe thunderstorm, and the plane ran into weather he could not handle. The plane broke up and crashed near Macon. All four on board were killed.

REX FUQUA

"Alan's death was devastating to Dad, as it would have been to any parent. I think my father in many ways had led a charmed life until Alan died. Not that there hadn't been a lot of struggles, but this was a real blow. The fact of the matter is, he never was a person who knew how to deal with his emotions well, so he simply withdrew."

Alan's death absolutely devastated me and destroyed much of my ambition. Parents are just not equipped psychologically to handle the death of a child. In our pain and agony over the loss of Alan, Dottie and I nevertheless felt sorry for the Macon air traffic controller whose carelessness caused the aircraft to crash. The evidence of this was so clear that the U.S. government paid the $100,000 maximum to the families of all four men killed in the accident. What a horrible memory the air traffic controller had to live with.

DOTTIE FUQUA

"J. B. had a difficult time dealing with Alan's death and, of course, you never get over something like that. He wouldn't go into Alan's room, he wouldn't talk about it. Talking about it was a release for me. I think he would have done so much more in business had that not happened. It was difficult for both of us because he wouldn't talk to me about it, and he just buried himself in his work."

As a memorial to Alan, we gave our church, Reid Memorial Church in Augusta, the Alan Fuqua Center, a youth facility that is used regularly. We also took over a site in the middle of Westover Cemetery in Augusta called the Alan Fuqua Meditation Garden, which serves as a haven for persons seeking peace and quiet in a beautiful setting. And, also in memory of Alan, we gave the Lovett School in Atlanta a $2 million performing arts center. Alan had graduated from Lovett in 1969 and had always had an interest in theater and music.

DEALING WITH DEPRESSION

Although Alan's death was the single most tragic event of my life, I have also had a chronic struggle over the years with severe depression. Most people do not know this, for I had never found it appropriate to reveal it before. I have suffered from this severe depression most of my adult life. In some ways, it seems useless to bring up my own depression now, since few men and women have the same severe type I do. But I know that depression, in all its many forms, strikes millions of Americans and is no longer the taboo subject it once was.

Although conventional wisdom might suggest that deep depression is only a temporary thing triggered by some incident in our lives, I can assure you that nothing could be further from the truth. Fortunately, there are many drugs these days (such as Prozac) that give good results for most people who have a relatively minor form of the disease. Unfortunately, my condition is more severe, and I have taken many different antidepressants over the years, usually without much benefit.

The good news is that I am in better shape now emotionally than I have been in recent decades, although I still take antidepressants daily. When I was at my worst, which was most of my adult life, I just wanted to sleep, or to escape reality.

Depressed people feel that nothing bad can happen when they are asleep. For many elders who did not grow up in the generation of modern medications, the words to describe depression do not come easily. By the very nature of the illness, your thoughts slow down and your thinking is clouded by indecision. You question even routine decisions, doubting your judgment as your thoughts slow to a snail's pace. You feel as though you have weights on your body and every movement is painful. Those around you cannot understand the overwhelming feeling of physical and emotional pain that accompanies this disease. Sleep is never restful and often punctuated with nightmares. Fatigue ensues, which only compounds the pain and self-doubt. Food becomes tasteless. Talking with friends and family can be overwhelming. You cannot work for more than a few hours and so avoid people. You become irritable for no apparent reason. This further isolates you both physically and emotionally. The pattern is a self-defeating spiral of guilt, isolation, and despair. Friends and family often arrange social events in an attempt to cheer you up. You feel guilty that you cannot enjoy their efforts and are embarrassed to be seen in this condition. It is difficult to appreciate the caring efforts of those around you. Eventually, family and friends who are closest begin to question your motivation, which increases your sense of self-doubt. Depression is an insidious disease. Society has traditionally judged depressed individuals harshly, believing that their problem is due to a weakness of character and laziness. Tragically, this only further limits people from seeking medical attention.

My depression was especially hard on my wife and children. I was antisocial for long periods and did not want to go to any functions. I would cancel business appointments for no good reason. I have been treated with everything that has come along over the past 50 years, including electroconvulsive therapy (ECT). I found ECT treatment to be little short of a miracle. In 1995 I took the electroconvulsive — or shock — treatment, and have been generally free of depression since that time. I know that shock treatments saved my life. In the past five years I am much improved. Shock treatment remains a controversial procedure, but it can be a highly effective last-resort treatment for those of us who don't respond to other methods such as drugs. Some old-fashioned psychiatrists still promote psychotherapy, but I simply cannot believe this method is effective in countering the effects of chemical imbalances that are the root cause of deep depression.

The treatment of mental illness is therefore a major interest of Dottie's and mine. I have invested over $4 million in philanthropic funds to promote the awareness of mental illness, especially in the elderly, and to suppress the stigma for its treatment. Hopefully, the stigma is declining as time passes. Taking an antidepressant pill should be no different from taking an antibiotic pill.

CHAPTER 25

REPAYING LOYALTY

I have always put a premium on loyalty. Perhaps it is because I had such an unhappy childhood, and I have therefore been grateful for every kindness I have since experienced along the way. Whatever the cause, I have always tried to repay those people who were kind to me over the years.

Lester Moody was the secretary of the Augusta Chamber of Commerce when I went there to get funding for my first radio station as a young man. Since I was a stranger, he could have easily turned me away, but he made some telephone calls and lined up financing from three people.

Years later, I learned that Moody had no retirement benefits and no health insurance. And, although he had done more for Augusta than anyone in recent memory, he was getting old and was in danger of losing his job. In 1962 I got myself elected as president of the Chamber in order to get a contract for him. I got Moody a modest pension and an employment contract, and when he got sick, I personally paid his hospital bill. And when the time came, I paid his funeral bill. Lester Moody had done so much for me, it was the least I could do for him.

One of the most important people in my early life was my seventh-grade teacher, Mrs. Alice Straw. She encouraged me when I was a lonely child, and I have always been grateful to her for her interest in me. She lived to be 107 years old and she spent the last part of her life in a nursing home. When I saw what nursing homes were like, it really shook me up, although I think she was in one of the better ones of that era. I thought it must be terrible to wake up and not have anybody around you that you knew, so I hired some ladies to be at her side for 24 hours a day for several years until she died. I also did little things for her, such as sending her 100 red roses on her 100th birthday. She appreciated the gesture and it resulted in a lot of publicity and conversation in the community.

LOYAL EMPLOYEES

I have always felt responsible for my personal employees and have treated them just as I treated employees of my corporations, especially with respect to such things as pensions. This has enabled, and will enable, some of them to retire and not have to work until they die.

Dottie and I had a yardman, Tessie "Bill" Johnson, who

served us in Augusta, and then again when we moved to Atlanta. I put aside money regularly in a special account for Bill. After working for more than 40 years for us, we retired him. The fund I had set aside for Bill enabled us to pay him a pension of more than we had paid him when he was working. At his death, there were enough funds to provide Bill with a respectable funeral. And Bill had willed the remainder of his funds to a relative who used the money to start a business.

In 2001, I retired Wilma Tinsley, my personal accountant for 20 years. Wilma knew more about my most personal business than anyone except myself. She will get a pension from me that, together with her Social Security and savings, gives her more income than she had while working.

I have provided for similar pensions and retirement funds for other key employees of mine, such as my chief pilot, Jim Keeton, and our housekeeper for some 28 years, Mary Nell Stanford. And the same policy applies to others.

When I reached the age of 60, I got a full-time driver because I thought it made no sense for me to be driving myself in the heavy Atlanta traffic. I often wonder why more business executives and affluent individuals in Atlanta don't have drivers. From a safety standpoint, it is well worth the cost. My driver and aide is Luther Latten, a well-educated black man who does several things besides drive. He goes with me everywhere I go. When I go out of town on overnight trips, I get a suite or a room with two beds so Luther can stay in one and I can use the other. At my age, I do not think it wise to travel alone.

Luther also prepares lunch for me in the dining room I have adjacent to my office. I have a serious hearing deficiency that causes me to avoid noisy places. As a result, I have lunch in my private dining room every day. We get food from various take-out places and restaurants, or we heat up frozen meals in the kitchen. Luther does an excellent job of selecting meals and serving them in a professional manner. I find this to be particularly worthwhile because I can have guests in to share lunch several times a week. I can get so much more out of a visit with a friend in my dining room where there aren't any exterior noises that affect my hearing. In addition, Luther knows far more about a computer than I do and keeps my computers running smoothly. Moreover, Luther is good company and fits right in with my friends. He has been a very loyal and valuable friend to me. It is only fair that I should look out for his best interests in the future to repay him for all his hard work and friendship.

I hear people talk about how well they treat their personal employees, but I think few put their money where their mouths are when it comes to loyal employees who get no corporate pension benefits.

ENRICHING THE EMPLOYEES

When the time came to sell WJBF Television, which had been my cash cow for many years, I decided I wanted to give a part of the company to certain employees who had been with me for a long time and who had made contributions to the profitability of the business. I wanted to do it on a tax-free basis, with capital gains taxes not being due until the business was sold in its entirety. Just giving these employees cash would have been impractical because of the income taxes involved.

I decided to set it up so that the employees would own 20 percent of WJBF. In effect I would give them stock in Fuqua Television, Inc., the corporation that owned WJBF. Here again, this was not an easy thing to do. The first step in my plan was to sell stock in WJBF to selected employees, who would pay for the shares with a loan from the bank. My plan was to issue new shares to the employees whom I wanted to reward based on longevity of employment and salary level. Employees did not have the money to buy the stock, so first I had to arrange credit for each one. I went to the Georgia Railroad Bank in Augusta and told them what my plan was, and that I wanted them to accept a note from each of the employees for the number of shares of stock times the value per share that we placed on this issue of stock. The corporation (WJBF) would guarantee the individual notes so the bank had little risk and loaned the money at the prime rate. It is important to place a fair value, but the lowest value you can come up with, on the shares of the corporation that the employee buys. The term of the note in this case was interest only for one year with a payoff over the next five years. This could be extended if necessary, but I expected it should be adequate time to execute the plan.

A minority interest in a private corporation is worth

very little, since it has no quoted market value and probably provides no dividend income as is true in this case. A minority stockholder in the real world is subject to the whims and desires of the majority stockholder(s). I used a value for the shares that was fair, but less than the pro-rata market value of WJBF if I were selling 100 percent of it. Keep in mind that the employees really got nothing of value until the execution of the rest of my plan.

The next step was to make this stock marketable without giving up my control of the company. Since these were shares in a private company, I wanted to swap these shares for shares in a public company. Here again, I had to find a listed company that I would get working control of together with my employees. In this way, the employees would end up with valuable stock with a price quoted in the paper every day.

After much research, I decided that the best prospect was a company called Central Foundry that was listed on the New York Stock Exchange. The only asset in the company was an old foundry in Alabama that was marginally profitable. It took several months, but we completed the deal. The end result was that the corporation that owned WJBF was acquired by (merged into) Central Foundry, and I became the dominant and controlling shareholder of Central Foundry. We changed the name to Gable Industries, and the listing remained on the New York Stock Exchange. This meant that WJBF employees had listed, readily marketable stock that was quoted in the paper every day. They became "insider" stockholders because of their affiliation with me as the controlling person and the need to make a filing with the SEC. We made a filing to have a "secondary" offering of shares and disclosed that the employee stockholders would sell sufficient numbers of their shares to pay off their notes at the Georgia Railroad Bank, which they all did. While the price that they sold for was far above what they had paid for the WJBF shares, I suggested they not sell additional stock as I had a plan for them to make much bigger gains, which was dependent on further financial moves.

Eddie Nicholson, the president I put in place at Gable Industries, set out to develop the company by buying other companies and sharply increasing its earnings per share. He was very aggressive and acquired several companies in a short time. The stock of Gable Industries soared. Keep in mind that Gable Industries had been WJBF and therefore the value of the shares the employee had through a merger of WJBF into Central Foundry were worth several times what they had paid for them. This is exactly what I had intended to happen.

Next we had another secondary offering to sell Gable stock to the public at the then-market price. I advised most of the WJBF employees to cash in their stock and diversify their assets because they were full-time employees of WJBF and they shouldn't be devoting their principal financial assets and their labor to the same company.

A majority of stock in the secondary offering was sold to European investors by the underwriters, Robinson-

Humphrey Co. This created a problem since, at that time, it was illegal for more than 20 percent of a radio or television station to be owned by non-American investors. We got out of this situation by separating Gable and WJBF into two classes of stock. There is no reason to explain how all of this was done, but the result was to put WJBF in a posture where it eliminated the foreign ownership and set WJBF up so it could be sold separately, which is what we proceeded to do.

Now the employees of WJBF and I had stock in two companies, Gable Industries and WJBF. Since Gable was growing much more rapidly than WJBF, and WJBF's stock price had declined sharply since it was mostly held in Europe, it made sense for WJBF to buy in and cancel its shares. So, WJBF made a public offer to purchase its own shares.

Now WJBF was back to where it was when I started this somewhat complicated plan, except that a group of employees now owned 20 percent of the company, which they had obtained with no cash and which had cost me nothing. I then proceeded to finalize the plan to enrich the employees by selling the whole corporation in a private transaction for $30 million.

BUTCH CAMPBELL, FORMER PRESIDENT OF WJBF-TV

"On our 25th anniversary of the TV station, we had a party in the Pinnacle Club in Augusta. I guess we had 35 or 40 people working at the station at the time, and he presented everyone with $1,000 just for the anniversary. In fact, he did make people millionaires. We were tickled to death. As I recall, he gave me 50 shares of stock. Just gave them to me. Frankly, I was very excited and appreciative, but I did not know what that meant. I don't think any of us did. I'm not sure he knew what the stock would ultimately be worth. As it turned out, it was a very large nest egg in my life and a lot of other people's lives. He was good about doing things like that for his employees."

When I sold the TV station, I did not sell the cable system. I sold the Augusta Cable System to Rex for $5 million, making a total value of the WJBF Corporation $30 million, of which the employees likewise received 20 percent, as that was their continuing share of ownership.

On the evening of the day that we closed the sale, I had a dinner at the Pinnacle Club in Augusta and passed out checks totaling $6 million, which represented the part of WJBF that the chosen employees had owned. It was interesting to see how the ten different employees handled their money. Some got almost a million dollars; they all got more money than they had ever expected to save. Several spent all of their money quickly; the others considered it to be retirement money. Those who turned theirs over to money managers did quite well with the bounty of their newly found wealth.

This is a good example of how a person can make a fortune for himself and at the same time provide opportunities for associates or employees. I came out of it with $24 million personally (80 percent of $30 million). I sold Gable separately to an English conglomerate for a handsome profit.

CHAPTER 26

THE IMPORTANCE OF A HOBBY

One of my regrets is that I never really learned to play. In my prime, I was always working to get ahead and I simply did not take time off to do things like play golf or go to sporting events. That is a great mistake in retrospect, and I now feel that a more balanced lifestyle would have been wise. I appreciate now the importance of having some recreational outlets outside of work. These distractions can lend you important perspective at times, and they encourage you to socialize outside your work circle.

I have never followed professional sports at all, to my regret. I have routinely turned down tickets to the World Series and other top sporting events in this country over the years because I knew I would not fully appreciate them. One true story that illustrates my lack of sports knowledge occurred when Dottie and I were at Bergenstock, a nice mountain resort in Switzerland, the day Hank Aaron set his famous home run record playing with the Atlanta Braves. We were attending a meeting of the branch of the Young Presidents Organization one joins after turning 50. Several people came up to me, knowing I was from Atlanta, and made remarks such as "You folks in Atlanta must be mighty proud of Hank." I finally had to ask someone who this Atlanta Braves player was. They were amazed that I had never heard of Hank Aaron and didn't know that he had just broken Babe Ruth's home run record.

LARRY KLAMON

"J. B. was in New York one time and somebody told him there was some sporting figure he ought to get and J. B. wrote down his name. Later we were at lunch and he said this guy had mentioned somebody we ought to get to endorse our products, but he had never heard of him. So he pulled out the piece of paper and handed it to me and it was Muhammad Ali. I said I'd take care of it. J. B. may not have recognized the names of these sports figures, but he understood the importance of celebrity promotion."

I probably should have learned to play golf, since so many people claim to have made such big deals while spending hours away from work. But I never took up the game because

I didn't think I had the time to be chasing a crazy little white ball around several miles of a golf course. Moreover, using golf carts isn't much exercise. Instead, I have spent a lot of my free time reading nonfiction books and magazines. I do not recall having read a novel of any kind in my adult life. I do not go to movies or watch movies on television, but this is because I have a serious hearing impediment. I was into computers early on, and I continue to enjoy this vast, amazing source of information. I get home delivery of three newspapers every day, and I subscribe to a whole host of magazines. I read rapidly and consume as much reading material in a month as the average person my age reads in a year. But that is only one sort of hobby.

As for recreational activities, my son Rex and I have found much enjoyment in our 1200-acre game preserve located an hour from Atlanta. It has a beautiful lodge that can sleep a lot of friends. We have one of the best-stocked fishing ponds around, and we have quail hunting supported by birds, dogs, trainers, and everything else that goes into that sport. We also have a professional skeet range and enough blinds and deer to ensure that one seldom fails if they are looking to shoot a deer with antlers. When I was growing up on the farm in Virginia, I never saw a deer, but now they are so numerous as to be a nuisance. The same is true for fish. Wildlife experts tell us that there are now more places to fish and more fish to catch than when Indians dominated this land 500 hundred years ago.

Until a few years ago, I was an avid hunter who would go almost anywhere to hear a gun shoot. For 15 or 20 years, I went to South Dakota for the opening of the fall pheasant season. A few of us would wait at the end of rows of corn while several hunters walked from the other end of the field toward the "standers." Some birds would fly as we walked toward them, but most of the pheasants ran ahead and did not rise from the field until they determined they were blocked at the end of the rows. It takes good eyesight to hunt pheasant this way because regulations require that only male birds can be shot. Fortunately for the hunter, the male pheasant is much more colorful than the hen.

REX FUQUA

"My father hunted as a boy, but I don't think he took it up again until he got into politics. Barbecues and quail hunting and dove hunting were very important aspects of politics in Georgia. One time we flew to northern Canada to hunt geese, and we went to this remote Eskimo village above the tree line where we stayed in Quonset huts. The accommodations were not up to his standards to begin with, and they had this Indian guide who got us up before daylight, which also was not his schedule. The guide proceeded to take us across the water in a small boat to this barren island where we were supposed to sit and wait for the geese to come over. Well, we lasted half a day, and Dad called for a plane to come get us."

I never went on a safari or into the mountains to shoot large game because I was primarily a wing shooter. I was an average shot, but I enjoyed going almost every year to Arkansas to shoot ducks. It was fun to take several friends with me in my airplane and fly in close to where we would hunt.

Aside from hunting, the only other passion I can claim during my lifetime is my love of flying. Airplanes have been probably the single most profitable thing I have used in my business dealings, as well as the source of much personal pleasure. I had dreamed of flying airplanes ever since I was a young boy on the farm and I would rush outside to look up at the sky whenever one came over.

I learned to fly in a Piper Cub when I was 19 years old in Charleston, and I continued to take more instructions after I went to Augusta. The Piper had a 35-horsepower engine and was little more than a kite with a motor. I was determined to be a really good pilot, and I advanced from one grade of license to the next, starting as a private pilot and going on to get a commercial pilot's license, then to a multi-engine license. When I got an instrument license, which certified I could fly on instruments without being able to see the ground, I was licensed to fly any kind of plane. The first plane I owned was a Taylorcraft that seated the pilot and one passenger — no room for baggage — and cost about $2,500. It had a bare set of instruments and a 65-horsepower engine. I really stepped up when I bought a used Beechcraft Bonanza. It was a single-engine plane that carried the pilot and three passengers comfortably. It was the only plane built that had a tail like a V. While the Taylorcraft made a speed of about 70 miles per hour, the Bonanza scooted along at about 140. Next came a new Piper Apache that had two engines, a speed of close to 200 mph, and plenty of instruments to fly in bad weather and at night. I had to live on a strict budget to save for these planes, but flying was the most enjoyable thing I did.

I especially enjoyed taking trips over the years with my family. My two boys loved Nassau, and we made many trips from Augusta to the Bahamas. We also flew to the West Coast in the late '50s and stopped at most of the national parks. We took along a 12-year-old friend to baby-sit. Dottie was never fond of flying, but she didn't complain.

One of my biggest thrills in the air came in 1964, when LBJ was running for president and I was invited to ride with him in Air Force One. Needless to say, I thoroughly enjoyed being able to say I had ridden in the number-one aircraft in the country. And I was not relegated to the back section, as Speaker of the House Newt Gingrich was by Bill Clinton!

I always tried to have the latest equipment on my planes, and I enjoyed instrument flying more than anything else I did for recreation. There was nothing to compare with the feeling of flying at night or in weather where you couldn't see anything. It was so exhilarating — I felt like I was the absolute master of the situation. I recall so well flying from Augusta to El Dorado, Arkansas, at night. (I had a television station in El Dorado.) At 8,000 or 10,000 feet on a clear night — and I always made this trip at night — I could see hundreds of gas flares from the oil wells in that area of the country.

It is difficult to explain what it is like to fly a plane to someone who hasn't done it. I always felt that I was the master of my destiny when I was behind the controls. In all the hours I have flown, I have had only one serious accident. This happened after I had bought a Lear jet and I had gotten out of the driver's seat and hired a pilot.

On this occasion, we were flying into LaGuardia Airport in New York at night when there was snow on the ground. The pilot, who was not accustomed to flying jets, made a number of errors. In the first place, he landed on the wrong runway. The second, more serious error he made was in landing too far down the runway to stop in a normal manner. The plane did not have reverse thrusters, so he put the brakes on and skidded off the runway. We made a 180-degree turn and the damage to the plane was considerable. I got out as the emergency crew rushed towards us and remember telling the pilot, "You'll never fly another airplane for me." Which he didn't. He was never able to make the transition to jet aircraft and was later killed in a helicopter crash.

There were other incidents that occurred during the thousands of miles I spent in my airplanes, but nothing as frightening to me as the landing at LaGuardia. As an experienced pilot, I usually remain calm when these things happen.

But that experience was not as frightening as one I had as a pilot. I had been invited to go duck hunting in Arkansas and was supposed to meet the other hunters in Memphis. I had a twin Bonanza, which was a medium-sized twin-engine propeller aircraft. When I started out, the forecast indicated there was to be some bad weather on the way, but I thought everything would clear up and I wouldn't have any difficulty.

The traffic controllers had ground radar that guided pilots around storms, but the radar in Memphis wasn't working. When I got close to Memphis and learned that the ground radar was out, there was no way for them to tell me which direction to go to get around the storm. I should have turned back, but I was so determined that I was going to go duck hunting that I decided to buckle myself into the seat, switch on the automatic pilot, and just ride right through the storm. A thunderstorm usually has a maximum diameter of five miles and you can ordinarily fly through it in a short period of time. That's what I did and it was the roughest ride I ever had. I got through it all right, but in retrospect it was a foolish thing to do.

The Memphis incident was scary, but I had another flying experience that was just plain embarrassing. I was in Augusta and had a V-tailed Bonanza at the time, which I loved, and I had just traded it for a new twin-engine Piper Apache aircraft that was going to be delivered on a Sunday. The day before was a beautiful afternoon, and I decided to take my Bonanza around the field one last time. I was circling Daniel Field in Augusta and a large group of people had assembled to watch the planes, including mine. I brought that Bonanza down in the prettiest landing I had ever made. The only problem was I forgot to put the landing gear down. Aircraft are made to withstand that type of mistake, and it's not a dangerous procedure to land without the wheels. It's just very embarrassing. On that airplane, you have a horn that sounds when you get too close to the ground without the landing gear down. In my excitement, I just didn't hear the horn.

Flying is always an adventure because you have to be prepared for any emergency. I remember taking off one morning when I was in the Legislature and heading for Atlanta in my airplane with our two sons and Carl Sanders's wife, Betty, on board. I figured there was something wrong because the gear didn't lock in place. When I got to Atlanta, I called the tower and said I had a problem, but I intended to land the aircraft anyway. They lined up all emergency equipment along the runway and I prepared for the most serious kind of accident. As it turned out, there wasn't anything in the world wrong with the plane, but we had some tense moments.

Even though I no longer fly myself, I have not given up my love for the activity. I now own a Canadair "Challenger," which is a big airplane with worldwide range. My chief pilot, Jim Keeton, has been with me for about 30 years and has carried me safely hundreds of thousands of miles. I now use my plane primarily to take my friends and myself on fun trips both in the U.S. and abroad.

For a birthday gift to myself, a group of friends and I flew from Atlanta to the North Pole and back. Now, there is nothing to be seen at the Pole except ice, and the only way we knew we'd been to the North Pole was when the pilots told us we were circling it. We made that trip in late June (my birthday is June 26), when the sun never sets at the North Pole.

ROBERT REDFEARN, FRIEND AND TRAVELING COMPANION

"If you're going to travel with J. B., be prepared to go first class. He's got a fantastic airplane that's so quiet you can hear conversations in flight. We stay in first class hotels and eat at the finest restaurants. He has a lot of imagination about the places we go to. When we went to the North Pole, the rest of us had no idea we were going there. The purpose of the trip was to go beyond the Arctic Circle. We went to the very northwestern tip of Canada and stayed at Inuvik, a little village with 2,000 people and the northernmost traffic light in the world. It was a lot of fun. We broke out a bottle of Dom Perignon champagne when we circled the North Pole."

Dottie and I made a trip with friends to Point Barrow, Alaska, once. That is as far north as the U.S. goes. Again we went near my birthday so we could talk with the folks who live in a place where there is no darkness in the summer and no daylight in the winter. Dottie and I have also made several trips to Europe, Russia, and South America over the years.

My buddies and I flew to Aruba Island off the coast of Venezuela in 1998 to see the last full eclipse of the sun in the western hemisphere for several decades. Of course, you can see it on television, but it's not like seeing the real thing when the sun is completely blocked out by the moon and it gets totally dark! We have made other trips in my plane, and it has been fun for a group of old men.

In 1999 we flew to Munich to see Oktoberfest, which was my fourth visit to that 200-year-old festival. We do one-day trips also, such as going to the Ford Museum in Dearborn, Michigan, and spending a day aboard a nuclear submarine. My plane only seats nine plus three crew, so not all my old friends can go on every trip we make. We have plans to make other trips over the next few years. These trips are fun for folks our age (all of us between 70 and 85) and are not strenuous.

CONCLUSION

20 THINGS THAT I HAVE LEARNED ALONG THE WAY

- I've learned that one never has a second chance to make a first impression.

- When I'm doing the talking, I'm not doing the learning.

- A temporary tolerance of mediocre performance leads to a permanent acceptance of poor performance.

- More money is made selling quality than in selling quantity.

- Opportunity is always temporary. . . . It must be either seized or lost.

- Don't confuse an education with wisdom — or college with an education. Education is something that will take you an entire lifetime — and you will still not be as educated as you should want to be. Whether you get to be an old person will be determined by whether you have had continuous curiosity.

- Successful people are successful because they take time out to think. Maybe you do your important thinking in the shower, on the golf course, or somewhere else. Most of the important planning and thinking in my career was done lying flat on my back in bed. Simply taking time out every day to do some serious thinking is the most profitable habit you can become addicted to.

- Oftentimes you think success is in the mind of your neighbor, your family, your friends, and your enemies, but really it's in your own mind. My own definition of success is doing the best you possibly can.

- Leaders prepare to recognize opportunities. The person who wants to feel the warmth of the sun stands on the south side of the tree — not the north side in the shade.

- One must first be ambitious to become a leader. Believe me when I say this makes it easier for you. There simply are fewer people out there really competing with you. Once you get up the first rung of the ladder of success, there are fewer people around you. But let me also suggest that on the way up, try to be nice to everybody. If you slip back down, you will meet some of the same people you passed on the way up.

- A higher return on effort comes from making good companies better than from trying to turn around the losers.

- I've learned that when people know that the results of

their efforts are being measured and appreciated, they try a lot harder.

- When people establish their own objectives, they are more committed to the achievement of those objectives.

- I can't predict the headlines on tomorrow morning's newspaper, much less forecast the economy, interest rates, or the stock market.

- I've learned that the best operating results are achieved when authority is delegated as far down the line as possible, where the action is.

- The difference in performance between the best people and the mediocre is a far greater difference than the additional compensation needed to hire the very best.

- I've learned that success comes from surrounding myself with people that are at least as smart as I am.

- I've learned you can't solve operating problems with staff from headquarters.

- The best predictor of a manager's future performance is his or her past record.

- I've learned that it is important to take the long view. . . . one day at a time.

COMPANIES CONTROLLED BY J. B. FUQUA
(OTHER THAN FUQUA INDUSTRIES)

as Chairman of the Board, CEO, Largest Shareholder
or otherwise Control of Management

NATCO CORPORATION

What Fuqua Industries, Inc., was called before the name was changed. It was a brick and tile manufacturer listed on the NYSE with sales of about $12 million and book value of about $10 million. I acquired 25 percent of Natco in 1965 in a complex transaction.

GREAT LAKES INDUSTRIES

This was a public company I had to gain control of and liquidate in obtaining control of Natco. It was traded OTC.

POLARIS CORPORATION

The first acquisition made by Natco-Fuqua Industries. A conglomerate created by a Milwaukee bank. A very important step in the development of Fuqua Industries, Inc.

CENTRAL FOUNDRY COMPANY

This company was listed on the NYSE. It was a cast-iron foundry in

Alabama that was subsequently renamed Gable Industries. Gable became the vehicle with which I merged WJBF-TV and acquired many other companies in a variety of industries.

GABLE INDUSTRIES
This company was a successor in name to Central Foundry Company. Listed on the NYSE. Gable made a lot of money for me personally.

VISTA RESOURCES, INC.
Rex and I acquired 40 percent of Vista for $12 million in 1989 with the plan that some of its cash would be used to acquire other companies. Vista's business was a profitable leather tannery in Maine. The cash that Vista had at acquisition was used to buy American Southern Insurance Company. Vista Resources later became Fuqua Enterprises, Inc. It then went into the medical products business, was merged with Graham-Field Health Products, and subsequently went into bankruptcy as a result of fraud. On paper we lost about $40 million.

FUQUA ENTERPRISES, INC.
See Vista Resources. Listed on the NYSE.

CMEI, INC.
This company was listed on the NYSE. Control was acquired by Fuqua Industries under a contract to develop CMEI and utilize its $150 million tax loss carry-forward.

PIER 1 IMPORT STORES
A national chain of specialty stores featuring merchandise primarily imported from the Far East. It was owned by CMEI, Inc., which was a REIT started by Tom Cousins. Fuqua Industries made a contract with Cousins to develop CMEI and use its tax loss carry-forward. Pier 1 Stores was the first significant acquisi-

tion of CMEI. The name CMEI was changed to Pier 1 Import Stores. Listed NYSE.

THE TRITON GROUP, INC.

Triton was acquired jointly by Fuqua Industries, Inc., and me and several other Fuqua Industries officers when it came out of bankruptcy. Triton was previously the Chase Manhattan Bank REIT. Its principal asset was property in Puerto Rico and a tax loss carry-forward of about $150 million. The Puerto Rico property was swapped for control of Simplicity Pattern Company.

SIMPLICITY PATTERN COMPANY

This was the largest ladies dress pattern company. It was a subsidiary of The Triton Group and was acquired by Triton in exchange for Puerto Rican property owned by Triton. It was listed on the NYSE.

RET INCOME FUND

RET was one of the two closed-end funds that had been invested solely in REIT stock that had been liquidated. It was one of the two companies that made up Cyprus Corporation. Its sole asset was cash.

SG SECURITIES, INC.

This company was listed on ASE. It had only cash when I acquired control. SG was merged with RET into Cyprus Corporation.

CYPRUS CORPORATION

This company was a successor in name of two closed-end investment funds, both listed on the ASE: RET Income Fund and SG Securities, Inc. These two funds had been at one time invested solely in REITs and had been liquidated. They were combined in the name Cyprus. Its sole asset was about $60 million cash. After getting Cyprus going, I sold my control position.

REPUBLIC CORPORATION

This was the former Republic Pictures Corporation that was big in the early days of the movies. It was a conglomerate that owned such things as a steel manufacturing company, a publishing company, and a post-production business serving the movie and television industries.

INTERSTATE MOTOR FREIGHT SYSTEMS, INC.

This company was headquartered in Grand Rapids, Michigan, and was listed on the NYSE. Control was acquired by Fuqua Industries through a purchase of a control position from the Trust Department of the Chase Manhattan Bank. It was a wholly owned subsidiary of Fuqua Industries for twelve years before its stock was distributed to Fuqua Industries stockholders.

HYTECH ENERGY CORPORATION

This company was a gas and oil development company headquartered in Midland, Texas. The company was the outgrowth of oil and gas properties owned by me that I had sold stock in to several dozen people. HyTech was merged into a company in a related field and subsequently into a NYSE-listed gas pipeline company.

BEAVER CREEK INDUSTRIES

This company was created in Iowa for the purpose of building a vodka distillery to use Iowa corn. This business plan was abandoned. I had a contract to develop the company and utilize its $3 million in cash to make a conglomerate. After the stock sold for wildly excessive prices, the contract to develop this company was transferred to another controlling party.

AMERICAN SOUTHERN INSURANCE COMPANY

This company was purchased from Prince Faisal via the U.S.

Department of Justice and merged into Vista Resources (subsequently Fuqua Enterprises, Inc.). Vista and Fuqua Enterprises were listed on the NYSE.

U.S. GUARANTY LIFE INSURANCE COMPANY

This company was created in 1956 by some friends and me. It operated for about two years and was then merged into another insurance company.

HONORS AND AWARDS

Through the years I have received many awards, all of which
I appreciate. Here is a listing of some of them:

- Horatio Alger Award
- Georgia State University Hall of Fame Award
- Shining Light Award, Atlanta Gas Light and WSB Radio
- The Caring Award, The Caring Institute
- Prince Edward Academy in Farmville, Virginia, was renamed The Fuqua School
- Fellow of the College Award, Capitol College
- Pinnacle Award, Sales & Marketing Executives International
- Philanthropist of the Year Award, The National Association of Fund Raising Executives

- Entrepreneur of the Year Award, Stanford Business School Alumni Association-Atlanta
- Alexis de Tocqueville Society Million Dollar Roundtable
- *Georgia Trend* 100 Most Influential Georgians
- Free Enterprise Medal as Entrepreneur of the Year, Shenandoah College
- Atlanta Entrepreneur Hall of Fame
- Georgian of the Year Award, Georgia Association of Broadcasters
- Philanthropist of the Year Award, The Georgia Chapter of the National Society of Fund Raising Executives
- Business Statesman Award, Harvard Business School Club
- Exceptional Service to the Community Award, The Christian Council of Metro Atlanta
- The Highest Effort Award, The Sigma Alpha Epsilon Fraternity
- Marketing Statesman Award, Sales and Marketing Executives International
- Outstanding Business Leaders Award, Northwood Institute
- Award of Merit for Distinguished Entrepreneurship, The University of Pennsylvania Wharton Entrepreneurial Center
- Duke University's business school was named The Fuqua School of Business
- Georgia Pioneer in Broadcasting Award
- American Academy of Achievement Golden Plate Award
- Augusta Junior Chamber of Commerce "Boss of the Year"
- President of the Augusta Chamber of Commerce
- President of the Augusta Exchange Club

HONORARY DEGREES

While I have a limited formal education, I have been awarded
honorary doctorates by ten colleges and universities.
Even if they don't represent any time in a classroom,
I am proud and flattered to have these certificates
to show on my office wall.

- 1995 Honorary Doctor of Humane Letters, Queens College, Charlotte, NC
- 1995 Honorary Doctor of Administration, Cumberland College
- 1991 Honorary Doctor of Laws, Mercer University
- 1991 Honorary Doctor of Laws, University of Tulsa
- 1990 Honorary Doctor of Humane Letters, Longwood College
- 1987 Honorary Doctor of Humane Letters, Queens College, New York City
- 1986 Honorary Doctor of Laws, Oglethorpe University
- 1982 Honorary Doctor of Humane Letters, Florida Memorial College
- 1973 Honorary Doctor of Laws, Duke University
- 1972 Honorary Doctor of Laws, Hampden-Sydney College

ACKNOWLEDGMENTS

Thanks to

W. Thomas Johnson, my good friend and confidant

Harry J. Middleton, Director of the LBJ Library,
for his editorial counsel

Scott Bard and Tysie Whitman of Longstreet Press,
for their vision and guidance

Don O'Briant,
for his partnership in this manuscript

Karen Heiser and Anne Sterchi,
for their good sense and collaboration

Grateful Appreciation to

All those who shared their memories for this book

INDEX